Forbidden Fruit

CHRISTIANE INMANN

Forbidden Fruit

A History of Women and Books in Art

PRESTEL
Munich · Berlin · London · New York

In memory of my mother Barbara Wieser

Acknowledgements

Throughout the five years I worked on this book, I have been indebted to no one more than Gregory Hedberg, who enthusiastically encouraged me from the time I first showed him a crude concept of the project. He read my first drafts and generously lent me his time and profound knowledge of art over all these years and urged me on with his quiet intelligence whenever I faltered or lost heart.

I also owe thanks to Claus Mueller who tirelessly spoke to the Italian Museums on my behalf, to Robert McInnes, Stephan Koja, and Susanna Allen, for their advice as well as to Patricia and Donald Oresman and all other private collectors whose artworks feature here.

This book has greatly benefited from the expert knowledge and archival material provided by Isao Okuda, professor emeritus of the University of the Sacred Heart, Tokyo, Ila Furman and Sarah Cash of the Corcoran Gallery of Art, Pat Boulware at the Saint Louis Art Museum, Margaret C. McKee at the Museum of Fine Arts, Houston, Julia Carver of Bristol's City Museum, Sandy Paci at DC Moore Gallery in New York, Betsy Kohut at the Freer Gallery of Art, Marie-Claude Saia at The Montreal Museum of Fine Arts, Jonathan Harrison at The Library of St. John's College Cambridge, Karen Lerheim and Gerd Woll at the Munch Museum in Oslo, Anita Duquette of the Whitney Museum of American Art, Sylvia Ferino-Pagden and Christine Surtmann at the Kunsthistorisches Museum Vienna, Gian Piero Cammarota at the Pinacoteca Nazionale di Bologna, the various departments at The Metropolitan Museum of Art, Laurie Chipps of The Art Institute Chicago, Maria Singer of the Yale Center of British Art, Joanna Hanna of the Springfield Museum, Jane Munro at the Fitzwilliam Museum, Cambridge, and Patrick Murphy at the Museum of Fine Arts, Boston; I sincerely hope I have not forgotten to mention anyone. I am indebted to all the museums whose artworks feature here for generously granting me the permission for reproduction.

The book would not have been possible without the generous support of the staff at Prestel, foremost Thomas Zuhr, who endorsed the project at first sight, Anja Besserer who answered all my questions with patience and eloquence, and Cilly Klotz. Special thanks go to Cynthia Hall, my tireless editor, who discussed many passages with me through red-eyed nights.

Contents

Introduction

Someone, I say, will remember us in the future.
Sappho, 640 B.C.

If—as the British philosopher Francis Bacon claimed—reading is nourishment for the mind and soul, it remained a forbidden fruit for women throughout much of history. The Sumerian scribes were already aware of the extraordinary power of literacy and jealously guarded its secrets. Patriarchal societies of all ages kept the knowledge of books and reading locked away from women and safeguarded the keys to this treasure chest, afraid that, if opened, it would become a Pandora's box.

Yet, women repeatedly figured as pioneers in the history of world literature, breaking through the barriers placed in their way to serve as enduring role models. The first recorded author in world history was a Sumerian princess who lived some 4300 years ago, and one of the greatest lyric poets of all time was Sappho. The world's first novel was also written by a woman, Murasaki Shikibu of Japan. In medieval Europe the ambers of knowledge were tended in convents by abbesses such as Ireland's Brigid of Kildare and Germany's Hildegard of Bingen. These, and many other, outstanding women's contributions to literary culture continue to be admired today.

Victor Hugo wrote that "to learn to read is to light a fire, every syllable that is spelled out is a spark," but for most women this fire remained a low and barely flickering flame until the emergence of more egalitarian and democratic societal structures. Reading generally remained an aristocratic privilege well into the age of Humanism. Even with the arrival of the printing press in 1454, books remained a rare commodity affordable only to a few; the reading material available to women was limited by the social and ethical standards of the day and consisted mainly of spiritual and devotional literature. An extensive command of the literary and visual tools necessary to decode and interpret cultural products was not among the skills patriarchal society encouraged women to develop. The consequences of this were clearly visible in their restricted roles in public life.

A woman's place was in the home, and any knowledge and competence necessary could be acquired there. Traditional paternalistic societies saw no need for women's formal education, let alone their broader intellectual engagement. In addition to the belief that education was counterproductive to a woman's traditional role, reading was considered only a thief of time, distracting a woman from her domestic responsibilities of nursing and raising children, running the household, and caring for her husband's well-being.

The advancement of educational opportunities took the form of a constant battle between the more progressive and conservative members of society. Spearheading the voices calling for change were outstanding, intelligent women who, sure of their intellectual gifts, rose above the disadvantages of their circumstances with courage, ambition, and determination, undeterred by serious risks to their reputations, by isolation, ridicule, and much worse. Female journalists were imprisoned; Gauguin's grandmother, Flora Tristan, ruined her health teaching the underprivileged and suffered a premature death; Hypatia and Olympe de Gouges both met violent death as a result of their convictions.

Each of these pioneering women—from different social backgrounds—carried the pursuit of knowledge a step further. Sympathetic and enlightened men who believed in women's intellectual capacity and their right to education became allies in these endeavors. Together, they created serious interest within the more enlightened and intellectual circles of their time, but, for the most part, such progressive impulses only resulted in concrete changes at a much later date. As early as 1405, Christine de Pizan eloquently argued that women's intellectual faculties were equal to those of men, but her *Book of the City of Ladies* remained without an echo for centuries. Almost four hundred years later Mary Wollstonecraft's powerful *Vindication of the Rights of Women*—a response to the eminent philosopher Jean-Jacques Rousseau's *Emile, or on Education*, which upheld traditional attitudes towards a woman's role—argued, among other things, for equal educational opportunities for women; it was greeted with downright amazement. It would take some hundred years until it began to be seriously considered, and it was not until the 1970s that she was granted her rightful place among the world's most progressive philosophical thinkers. Innumerable women who worked for the same cause, but have remained unknown, take their place alongside these very visible protagonists. While the impact of these extraordinary women's efforts may have initially been quite limited, they nonetheless succeeded in paving the way for the common woman's progress.

As with any kind of power, the privileged classes were the first to benefit from the fruits of literacy and the knowledge it entailed. In medieval Europe, scholarly pursuits took place under the auspices of the Church and, even for most aristocratic girls, having access to books and pursuing knowledge beyond the domestic arts meant joining a convent, one of the few places where higher learning was available to women. Secular education for women began in the Renaissance, but long remained a luxury reserved for the elite. Great and talented women such as the poet Vittoria Colonna or the painter Sofonisba Anguissola flourished within the enlightened humanist circles of Renaissance Italy.

Around the 1640s, constant technical improvements led to an expansion of book printing throughout Europe and saw an unprecedented increase in literature catering to the early-modern woman reader. While the majority of these books were still devotional in nature, literate, well-to-do women now had access as well to some geography books, travel narratives, belles letters, and plays. In the early eighteenth century a diverse selection of reading material helped to create a culture of reading for women that found its most distinctive form in the literary Salons of Rococo France. These were dominated by wealthy, well-educated women; however, many considered this culture of reading more a frivolous indulgence than a serious pursuit of knowledge. All these developments bypassed the average woman, who had neither the means to buy books nor the skills or time to read them. Until the early to mid-nineteenth century, the education of the common girl took place primarily at home and was generally limited to a rudimentary knowledge of the alphabet, some arithmetic, and the skills necessary for her domestic duties and other labors.

Even when public schools were established, the curricula for boys and girls differed substantially. The belief in the necessity of a separate class of literature for women persisted until well into the nineteenth century and was reflected in the written material provided for them. Whereas men's access to reading material was unlimited, women were given devotional and instructive texts, some travel literature, light biographies, and morally uplifting or recreational literature written by authors whose ethical credentials were unquestionable. Women of letters were expected to write for the woman reader; this meant "suitable" works focusing on women's lives and the domestic sphere, steering clear of serious matters such as politics, philosophy, and scholarship. Crossing this clear-cut division could have dire consequences.

The male establishment feared women's intellectual liberation and what it regarded as the potentially subversive effects of the written word. A woman's mind, it was argued, was too delicate to be exposed to outside influences; her thoughts could easily be manipulated, leading to disastrous consequences in the form of independent ideas and opinions. As a result, it was standard practice for husbands and fathers to select the material read by women. The sentiment expressed by the Korean proverb that "words are seeds" was clearly at the root of such fears. The notion that a woman could have an innocent passion for intellectually stimulating material was so foreign that any woman reading academic and scholarly literature was suspected of having a hidden agenda. But mothers worried too, fearing the loss of their daughter's virtue and grace. Even in the best circles, a well-read, bookish girl was met with suspicion. Too much worldly wisdom, let alone any display of it, was not considered a desirable trait in a woman. Venomous remarks about the so-called virago, an abusive term for bookish women, were used to discourage women's intellectual interests; more innocuously, it was claimed "that reading not only wrinkles the mind but also the face"!

There was general consensus that it was acceptable for women to both read and write poetry; poems were considered to have more moral clarity than other texts. This was even a cross-cultural phenomenon: For the women of China's Han Dynasty, the court ladies of Japan, and even the young slave Phillis Wheatley in colonial America, poetry was an appropriate form of literary indulgence. Novels, in contrast, were long regarded as particularly dangerous because the woman reader's possible "real life" identification with their characters could lead her to flights of fancy and distract her from her duties. This was particularly true, it was believed, of French novels; moralizing Dutch and German novels were more acceptable, and the American novel for the most part posed little to no threat.

Despite the persistence of suspicion about women's reading, between 1850 to 1900 women had established a certain independence in their choice of reading material, attributable in part to industrialization and the accompanying increase in wealth and their greater access to higher education. This breakthrough came earlier in countries with a more egalitarian political structure where widespread literacy was considered a prerequisite of the democratic process. The United States led the way in the founding of women's colleges: For example, 799 students were enrolled at Vassar College by 1900 while Oxford's first women's college, Lady Margaret Hall, had a mere 17.

A far more liberal attitude towards women's access to books and other reading material made steady progress thereafter. What had been an exclusively aristocratic privilege became an increasingly democratic activity. Once women realized the empowerment and joy of knowledge, and once the educated woman's benefit to society and potential for self-improvement was recognized, there was no turning back. One telling example of how weak men's attempts to control women's reading had become was their insistence on separate reading rooms in libraries that had opened their doors to women. Women, men complained, disturbed the seriousness of such august institutions; they rustled their clothing, giggled, gossiped, and even flirted within its walls. But this barrier, of course, soon fell.

The intention of the present book is to recall the long and difficult struggle of women's encounters with books throughout history. By juxtaposing a historical overview of the path women have forged with evocative images of them and their books, it offers a series of insights into the changing circumstances of women's access to reading and education over four millennia. Chronologically arranged, the volume opens in the ancient world, exploring civilizations as diverse as Mesopotamia, classical Greece, and China, traveling through the European Middle Ages and Renaissance to modern England and America. In the cultures discussed here, this achievement has become so self-evident that—in the twenty-first century—it is scarcely visible any longer. But this democratic right has still not been won for the many women throughout the world whom poverty and oppression force to remain in intellectual darkness.

Each of the four chapters that follow briefly outlines the development of women's access to reading material and examines it in light of images of women from the periods discussed, the books they read, and the worlds they inhabited. The paintings speak in different aesthetic vocabularies and within different visual traditions; they raise questions and offer clues. Some of them are representative of an entire historical era, others reflect on a particular moment in time with detailed intensity; all illuminate the different meanings of the act of reading by a woman. They are far from a complete or unbroken history, however; nor are they used here as simple illustrations of the broader historical patterns. Instead they offer a window into the development of reading over the ages and the evolution of new attitudes towards the intellectual and social advancement of women in various regions and cultures.

The nature of the books depicted in these images is significant, for it demonstrates the ways in which books as objects have been endowed with a wide variety of meanings, as symbols of piety, privilege, luxury, virtue, temptation, or leisure. In these works, what a sitter is reading—and even the act of reading itself—is central to her identity and an indication of her socio-economic background, her status within society, her attitude, and character.

The paintings also permit insights into the individual artists who created them, into her or his personal interpretation of, and particular approach to, the subject matter. Towards the beginning of the twentieth century, formal developments increasingly take the foreground; the final chapter looks at how the works' visual and formal means of expression relate to their larger cultural context. In the selection of works priority was given to the sitter's or artist's relevance within the broader development of women's educational opportunities, and the cultural and historical significance of the book depicted in the painting. Placed side by side, these paintings make remarkable statements about a woman's place within her society; many of the works directly or indirectly tell the story of women who were able to prevail over societal constraints. The present book is intended to encourage looking at paintings of women reading with renewed curiosity and to be an inspiration for the activity of reading. In short, it is a homage to the art of painting and reading and to women's long journey to achieve the freedom to read.

“Those Who Can Read, See Twice As Well”

MENANDER, FOURTH CENTURY ATTIC POET

First Steps: From the Cradle of Civilization to the Middle Ages

THE ANCIENT WORLD

It may come as a surprise to many readers that the first author known by name in world literature is a woman. There had been scribes before her but Princess Enheduanna (ca. 2285–2250 B.C.) was the first to sign her cuneiform tablets by name, thus establishing her identity as an author 4300 years ago. Enheduanna was the daughter of Sargon, King of Akkad and conqueror of Sumer, who strategically appointed her high priestess at the major temple in Ur in order to support his political ambitions. His reign resulted in the unification of northern (Akkad) and southern (Sumer) Mesopotamia and he placed his Akkadian daughter at one of the centers of Sumer, at Ur, and also gave her a distinct Sumerian name. Enheduanna means "priestess, fitting for heaven." In her prestigious role as *entu*-priestess of the moon god Nanna, she acted as the embodiment of the goddess Ningal, the divine consort of Nanna. Enheduanna "could reveal his secrets and deliver oracles in his name." Her temple hymns praised Sargon's wise rule, and her poems, as well as the incantations to the goddess Inanna ("The Exaltation of Inanna"), constituted an unmatched literary achievement until the time of Sappho.

During the reign of Sargon, the Assyrians experienced a golden age in which the arts, including sculpture, reached new heights. One example of this is the visually masterly balanced, elegantly carved and inscribed alabaster disk, excavated in several fragments in the area of the inner sanctum of the temple of Ur (page 24). That the disk is shaped like a moon is obviously no accident. The team of archeologists that unearthed the disk included members from Britain and the University of Pennsylvania Museum Expedition of 1925–26. Now in that institute, the disk pictures Enheduanna together with three attending priests. The princess stands second in line, wearing a long tufted garment and the *aga* (a rolled brimmed cap).

The script too displayed a high level of skill in the writing of cuneiform signs. Enheduanna's hymns, composed in Sumerian, were found in thirty-five cities throughout Babylonia. Control of the office of priestess was of such political, economical, and ideological importance that for the next five hundred years, every ruler installed his daughter or daughters as high priestess in Ur or other Babylonian cities. The rulers were aware of the extraordinary power of the written word, and reading and writing were reserved for the power holders.

In Greek antiquity, Athenian women of noble lineage were not only literate but also educated in the arts, which included dance, music, and singing. Poetry was especially

1 The Poetess Sappho, seated
Red-figure vase by the Polygnotos workshop, ca. 440–430 B.C.
National Archeological Museum, Athens

This red-figure vase depicts the poetess Sappho reciting one of her poems to music before a group of three of her students. Originally created for the practical needs of transportation and storage of spices, wine, and other commodities, vases later developed elegant and specific shapes and became an integral part of the Greek dinner and drinking banquets immortalized by Plato. Sappho's representation as a "reader" on this vase indicates her extraordinary status, for in general women were depicted as muses, dancers, or musicians but never in a connection with philosophical activity.

important, and educated women actively participated in religious cults as priestesses, visionaries, and poets. The greatest poetess of all antiquity was Sappho (page 26, fig. 1). Born into an aristocratic family around 600 B.C., she lived and worked mainly in her hometown of Mytilene, an

In Greek antiquity, women of noble lineage were not only literate but also educated in the arts.

important cultural center on the island of Lesbos. It is not known if her passionate lyrical songs and her hymns to the goddess Aphrodite were copied by scribes nor how they were circulated in her lifetime. In the era of Alexandrian scholarship (the third and second centuries B.C.) her work was compiled into nine books; some 200 fragments and a complete song have survived. Of her music nothing remains. Sappho's romantic poetry was directed toward female students who gathered around her singing of women's feelings and experiences, in the Greek tradition of older women mentoring and educating promising younger students. In this way, women's knowledge, whether of the social graces, music, poetry, or philosophy, was passed down through the generations. As women's freedom was later drastically curtailed in Greek society Sappho's work was shunned and even came to be seen as immoral. The earlier independence and expressive freedom of the teacher from Lesbos and her students was no longer acceptable for proper Greek women. Sappho is an iconic cultural figure whose work has never ceased to fascinate readers. Even today she remains the subject of scholarly research. Her poetry has been repeatedly translated, interpreted, and reinterpreted by great scholars throughout the ages. Her image is found in numerous works of art, including painted vases, frescos, and paintings. A particularly fine example of the latter is Gustav Klimt's *Sappho* of 1888–90, now at the Historisches Museum in Vienna.

Literacy among Greek women was not widespread. Those few from culturally sophisticated environments who commanded a good knowledge of reading would have had access to Greek novels such as *Chariton and Chaereas*, and *Daphnis and Chloe*, both stories of love and adventure with a complicated plot and the precursors of the romance novel. The great Greek epics were the domain of men.

Ancient Rome prided itself on providing education to women. The Romans, like the Greeks, considered an educated wife and daughter an asset to the family's well-being. Schooling for girls (and boys) from wealthy households (schools charged tuition fees) started at the age of seven and elementary schools existed even in smaller villages. At the age of thirteen, successful pupils could enroll in secondary schools, and approximately twenty existed in Rome around A.D. 130, but only a minority of girls attended those. An elite girl's lessons would include classes in Greek and Latin, reading poetry, and some study of more complicated texts. The education of non-aristocratic girls was, if at all, basic, with a curriculum of reading, writing, and some arithmetic.

Roman women, however, remained strictly under the guardianship of their husbands, and their public activities were generally limited to the religious sphere. (The vestal virgins enjoyed a high status). Countless artworks from the time—portraits, busts, relief sculptures, mosaics, and pottery—depict women participating in religious rites. Women's literary activities were restricted to writing poetry (page 26). The educated wife received no recognition beyond her role as a status symbol for her husband. There were many powerful women throughout Roman history, such as Livia Drusilla (58–29 B.C.) or Agrippina the Younger (A.D. 15–59), but nothing is known about the extent of their education.

In the cultural and intellectual capital of antiquity, Alexandria, the Greek mathematician and philosopher Hypatia (ca. A.D. 370–415) took the stage as a symbol of learning. Initially she taught at her house, where she assembled pupils around her in a manner that would first be seen again in the salons of eighteenth-century Europe. Around A.D. 400, she became head of the Neoplatonist school of philosophy in Alexandria, and students traveled from far and wide to attend her classes. All her writings have been lost but entries in a tenth-century encyclopedia, *The Suda Lexicon*, state that Hypatia wrote a thirteen-volume work on the *Arithmetica* of Diophantus.

Hypatia's legendary beauty and extraordinary life inspired a number of artists, writers, and painters alike. In 1885, the English Pre-Raphaelite Charles William Mitchell (1854–1903) painted her in a dramatic pose—she is portrayed standing naked in front of an alter (referring to her murder in a church), her body covered with her long, flowing blond hair, her look suggesting that she is ready to sacrifice herself for knowledge and science. The Victorian writer Charles Kingsley (1819–1875) also devoted himself to the pagan intellectual in his "Hypatia or New Foes with an Old Face" that was published as a series in *Fraser's Magazine* in 1852–3. Hypatia's great philosophical and political influence ultimately led to her brutal murder at the hands of a Christian mob. According to contemporary accounts, she was skinned alive and torn to pieces. After Hypatia's death many scholars and students left Alexandria for Athens, the center of mathematics at the time, marking the beginning of Alexandria's cultural decline.

CHINA AND JAPAN

Some 300 years earlier, on the other side of the world in China, the gifted Ban Zhao (A.D. 45–ca. 115) was the first female Chinese historian (page 28). She produced her work during the Eastern Han Dynasty, A.D. 25–200, an era marked by respect for women's wisdom and literary learning (if only for the purpose of bringing up good sons). A large number of high-ranking women were fully literate and "actively educated their daughters to equip them with the profound moral wisdom that was locked away in the written word."

Ban Zhao took over the task of completing the *Book of Han (Han Shu)*. The project had been started by her father, an eminent historian. Following his death, the work was continued by his son Ban Gu, who fell victim to a politically motivated murder. Ban Zhao was then expressly summoned by the emperor He Di to compile, edit, and complete the unfinished work—a monumental task that took her some fourteen years. *The Book of Han*, a record of the Dong (Western) Han Dynasty, is China's first book of dynastic history and became the foundation for all future works of this kind.

Born into a family of scholars, Ban Zhao enjoyed a diversified education provided by her mother (in the "domestic arts") and father (in history, philosophy, and classic literature). An avid reader of classical works, she developed a great interest in women's social roles. One result of this concern was *Admonitions for Women* (*Nüije*), a conduct book for women's daily life in which Ban Zhao strongly recommended female education. But however advanced the recommendation, in principle the *Nuije* nonetheless adhered to the Confucian feudal restraints imposed on women, a fact that led to her high esteem within the country's traditional male intellectual circles, who "canonized her as China's greatest female scholar." As a guidebook and moral compass, it has influenced Chinese gender socialization into the twentieth century.

Although she claimed to have written *Admonitions for Women* for her daughters to prepare them for marriage, the book was really intended for a much wider female readership. With its masterfully disguised phrasing, the *Nüije* was a kind of survival manual for married women living in their husband's households and a guide to fending off intrigues and plots to eventually reach positions of power themselves. Ban Zhao also gave lectures at the imperial library, teaching the highest ranking court ladies, proving that it was possible for a gifted woman to rise to the position of teacher and tutor at the imperial court. It is said that the dowager empress Deng Su—Ban Zhao had been her tutor in astronomy, mathematics, history, and Confucian classic—thoroughly mourned Ban Zhao's death. These achievements made Ban Zhao a role model for women who aspired to such positions in the centuries to come. Other educated and talented Han dynasty women wrote essays and poems, both socially acceptable forms of literary indulgence, for, with the exception of the incomparable Ban Zhao, serious philosophy and scholarship remained the realm of men.

Almost a millennium later, further east in Japan, learned ladies of the court were active readers, and some great writers would emerge from among their ranks. Sei Shonagon (ca. 968–ca. 1025, page 30), who was in the service of the Empress Teishi (also called Sadako), wrote *The Pillow Book* based on her observations of courtly life over an entire decade. Written in the style of a diary, *The Pillow Book* is marked by great sensitivity and exceptional wit and its amusing chapters bear titles such as "Things that Arouse a Fond Memory of the Past" or "Hateful Things." Subtle and sophisticated, at times sad and then again humorous, *The Pillow Book* found its main readership among ladies of the court and the wives and daughter of courtiers. The first printed version appeared on the book market in the seventeenth century and its "linguistic purity" and vivid collage of Japanese court life is still admired by readers today. *The Pillow Book* is considered the best contemporary document of life at the refined Heian court (784–1185), a period in Japanese history that set standards in aesthetics and culture that endured long after it had relinquished its power to the samurai.

Sei's contemporary and erstwhile rival Murasaki Shikibu (ca. 973–ca. 1015) would write the world's first novel, *The Tale of Genji*, generally considered the ultimate masterpiece of Heian literature. The personalities of these two eminent writers were quite different. Sei had a natural wit coupled with a certain arrogance, whereas Murasaki was very composed and earnest. Tutor and companion to Empress Soshi, the noble Murasaki came from a family of poets and writers. Girls of noble background who were expected to become members of the court were carefully educated. They had access to a variety of books including Chinese literature, which was, however, considered unladylike to read. For this reason Murasaki tried to hide her knowledge of Chinese and, like other contemporary women writers, composed her works in a Japanese script generally understood by her aristocratic readership.

The Tale of Genji (*Genji monogatari*), about a fictitious prince of the same name, was written by Murasaki between 1001 and around 1010 and is interwoven with accurate details of the unique society in which Murasaki lived. One of the greatest works of Japanese literature from the Heian period to the present, *The Tale of Genji* has been treasured by more Japanese readers than any other literary work. It has also become a classic of world literature, and continues to be reprinted in various formats and luxuriously illustrated editions. Japanese art has depicted scenes from Murasaki's work ever since it was written (page 32); in fact, no other work of Japanese literature has inspired more illustrations, many of them as beautiful as visual poetry.

The Heian era (794–1185) represented a golden age of Japanese literature in which writing in the vernacular experienced its first great flowering. Women writers produced nearly all the important literature of this period and popularized the art of Japanese prose. Sophisticated in style, these works appealed to readers because of their more accessible writing system known as *hiragana*, which consisted of a simple alphabet or syllabary (derived from Chinese characters). The writing style of men was a rather stiff prose, generally composed in classical Chinese, the language of the bureaucracy. Women' literary works were more successful than those of their male contemporaries not only during their authors' lifetimes, but they have retained this status until today.

As in other contemporary cultures, women writers in Japan wrote primarily for a readership of educated, aristocratic women and, as in other contemporary societies, most non-aristocratic women remained illiterate. Thus the great wealth of literature from the Heian period was written by the aristocracy, about the aristocracy, and for the aristocracy. Japanese noblewomen had access to books but obviously not enough because, according to legend, it was the empress herself who asked Murasaki to write a "new" story to enrich their "limited" library. The masses had to wait some 600 years before the printing press made her masterpiece available to them.

THE EUROPEAN MIDDLE AGES

For both women and men, literacy in Europe during the Middle Ages centered on the consumption and production of religious texts. Most women readers, such as Matilda of Tuscany (1046–1115)—best known for her support of Pope Gregory VIII during the Investiture Controversy that resulted in the famous barefoot penance of Emperor Henry IV at her castle at Canossa in January 1077—were still of aristocratic descent. Matilda's unconventional upbringing for a girl of the eleventh century and her degree of education are reflected in her keen acquisition of manuscripts and her patronage of the arts. In the *Vita Matilda* of around 1116 (the biography of a woman was in itself something unique in the twelfth century), her biographer Donizone records that she read and spoke Latin, as well as the vernaculars of German, French, and Italian. She read the Gospels, St. Augustine, and probably some classical writers, such as Virgil (who was also born in Mantua). Matilda donated her manuscripts to the monasteries she was associated with, such as San Benedetto Po near Mantua and Nonantola, near Modena, where some are still preserved and on public display for interested readers, as is one in the Morgan Library in New York.

In many ways, including intellectually, the Middle Ages remained a dark age for women. For much of society, opportunities for intellectual development were severely limited and intellectual curiosity—particularly women's—was seldom encouraged. Most medieval people never learned to read beyond the rudimentary ability necessary for everyday activities. Access to books and choice of reading matter was extremely limited, strictly controlled, and carefully sanctioned by religious and secular authorities. Because opportunities to learn to read—whether in school or privately—were so limited, and the costs of books so prohibitive, most people remained illiterate.

Most medieval people never learned to read beyond the rudimentary ability necessary for everyday activities.

For medieval women, access to books meant joining a convent. It was common practice to send girls of noble descent to convents run by the many religious orders. Throughout the Middle Ages, it was here, in the monasteries and convents, that the embers of literacy were kept aglow. In fifth and sixth-century Ireland, for example, scribes tirelessly copied Greek, Roman, and Hebrew texts, and their so-called white martyrs traveled throughout Europe bringing with them books, learning, and a desire for knowledge. Irish missionaries founded many of the continent's most important monasteries and libraries, such as Fontaines, Luxeuil, St. Gall, and Bobbio. Early on, the Irish appointed nuns as abbesses, of whom Brigid of Kildare (ca. 451–525) is the most famous. She founded two monastic institutions—one only for women—and also established an art school that concentrated on metalwork and manuscript illumination.

Since books were most frequently produced by monks and nuns who copied sacred, scientific, philosophical, and other texts, monasteries held the largest book collections. These handmade books were often works of art themselves, ornamented in gold and silver and containing exquisite illuminations in brilliant colors of unsurpassed beauty. Text and illumination were often meant to complement each other, mutually enriching one another in complex ways. The production of any manuscript was a laborious process and it often took years to create a single illuminated volume. They were sometimes bound with elaborate covers, adorned in gold, silver, and precious stones and clasps, thus adding even more to their value. It was not unknown for such a book to be traded for a piece of land. Outside of the monastic world, such valuable books were only owned by the most wealthy and powerful members of medieval society. The average woman (or man) did not possess even the most modest undecorated book.

One of the most remarkable women of universal learning in the Middle Ages was the German mystic Hildegard of Bingen (1098–1179, fig. 2). Known as the "sibyl of the Rhine," the abbess Hildegard was a writer, composer, and a natural scientist. At the age of eight, Hildegard was sent as a tithe to a convent, took the monastic vow when she was sixteen, and was elected abbess in 1136. Many women writers in the Middle Ages were abbesses, but Hildegard was the first nun on the European continent to teach and preach publicly. Her holistic approach to human existence, spiritually and physically, made her an authority on many aspects of life in the eyes of her contemporaries, and she traveled throughout Germany to reach people from all walks of life. Her broad knowledge and charismatic personality made her a consultant to several kings and queens, including Emperor Friedrich Barbarossa, King Henry II of England and his wife Eleanore, and also to popes, bishops, abbots, and abbesses. She corresponded frequently with all of them, and these letters constitute a central part of her surviving work.

Hildegard's most important work is the *Scivias*, in which she records her mystical visions. Her treatises on natural history and medicine are presently experiencing a remarkable revival of interest. It was Hildegard of Bingen who discovered the health benefits of detoxifying diets, for example. She died on 17 September 1179 at the Rupertsberg Monastery near Bingen, after having spent seventy-three of the eighty-one years of her life in a monastery.

2 Hildegard of Bingen
Illustration from the Lucca Codex
Liber Divinorum Operum,
ca. 1220–30
Bibiloteca Statale, Lucca

In the *Liber Divinorum Operum, or Book of Divine Works*, written in 1151, Hildegard of Bingen expounds her theology of man being the peak of God's creation. It is considered her most important work.

Hildegard's contemporary, Eleanor of Aquitaine (ca. 1122–1204, fig. 3), was the wealthiest—and possibly most powerful—woman of the twelfth century. Of legendary beauty and grace, Eleanor was queen consort of both Louis VII (1137–1152) and Henry II (1152–1204). Raised at one of Europe's most cultured courts, she was well educated, extremely competent, and decisive. After having her first marriage to King Louis II of France dissolved by means of a clever plot, her second marriage to Henry of Anjou, eleven years her junior and later King Henry II of England, was a union of love rather than a dynastic or socio-political arrangement, even though Eleanor was a highly political person.

Also a patron of the arts, Eleanor made her court at Poitiers into a center of poetry and music, and especially of the art of the troubadours. Her grandfather, Guillaume IX, is considered the first troubadour in history and laid the cultural foundation upon which Eleanor built. Troubadours were lyric poets who founded the literary tradition of *amour courtois*, or courtly love, referred to as such in literary history since 1876. Worldly rather than religious in nature, courtly love poetry was the most significant lyric form of the twelfth and thirteenth centuries. Initially performed at court for the aristocracy, in the thirteenth century this literature was carried to country taverns and inns through singing and verse by around a hundred traveling troubadours—including some twenty women. The lyrics of courtly love romanticized and idealized women, and sponsorship of this art form is mainly associated with women, such as Ermengarde, viscountess of Narbonne (d. 1196) and Comtesse Marie de Champagne (d. 1198).

The production of manuscripts began to increase around A.D. 1200. Books were now often made in smaller and less luxurious formats, which allowed for a slightly wider distribution. But books available to women were still very limited in number and in content. Chiefly religious or instructive in nature, they were intended to be read repeatedly and regularly, and to be learned by heart for recitation. This is exemplified in the popular book of hours, which, in the late Middle Ages, was quite often the only book even relatively wealthy people owned. The book of hours was a devotional tome, containing a collection of prayers and meditations appropriate to the seasons, months, days, and hours. Each book of hours was unique and often contained regional variations reflecting the saints revered in a particular area. Some books of hours were exquisite and precious objects and popular as wedding presents. Simpler versions were used in the education of children.

3 Tomb of Eleanor of Aquitaine, detail
Fontevrault, ca. 1204

Eleanor of Aquitaine's court at Poitiers was a center of troubadour poetry, the most significant literary form of the twelfth and thirteenth centuries. Raised at one of Europe's most cultured courts, Eleanor became a great patron of the arts and literature. Her likeness is carved on the lid of the tomb with the inscription "for eternity," where she is depicted reading a Bible. Her culture, independence, strength, and determination served far beyond her lifetime as an example for women of all social classes.

The twelfth, thirteenth, and fourteenth centuries saw the rise of the knightly tale, a literature of heroes and miracles, magicians, dragons, and other fabled animals. Courtly women most certainly had access to manuscripts of stories from the Arthurian legend with its famous sorceress Morgan Le Fay and Merlin the magician, as well as so-called beast epics such as that of the trickster Reynard the Fox, among other works. But, in general, for the next 200 years or so, most women's reading activities and their access to reading material remained highly restricted. The Enlightenment was still centuries away, but the voice of one herald could already be heard.

This was the voice of Christine de Pizan (1364–1429), considered the first female crusader for women's rights and the most versatile und successful writer of her time. She famously argued that if it were customary to send little girls to school and to teach them the same subjects as boys, they would learn just as fully and would understand just as much. Devoted to the protection and defense of women's virtue and capabilities, she argued with reason and logic for women's access to education in works such as *The Book of the City of Ladies* (1405). In its sequel, *The Book of Three Virtues* (1407), de Pizan writes about domestic life and the role of women in early fifteenth-century France, a subject that has begun to be adequately appreciated only by present-day historians.

Christine de Pizan was born in Venice and at the age of four moved with her family to France, where her father had taken up an appointment as astrologer and physician at the court of Charles V (called "the Wise," 1364–1380). The foundation for de Pizan's remarkable career was laid by her father, who provided her with a humanist education, which she herself refined over the years through intensive and extensive reading. Widowed at a young age (her husband died in 1389), de Pizan was one of the first women in history to support herself and her three children by the pen (page 34). Her initial success with her lyrical ballads and poetry dates from the mid-1390s and earned her several famous readers and patrons, such as the French queen Isabeau de Bavière and her ladies-in-waiting, as well as the Duke of Orleans and Philip the Bold, who commissioned her to write a biography of Charles V. Deeply rooted in France, de Pizan declined an invitation by Henry IV of England to work at his court. However, in despair over the political developments in her adopted country she eventually gave up writing and retreated in 1418 to the monastery of Poissy, joining her daughter who had been residing there as a nun since 1397. She broke her literary silence only once in 1429 to eulogize Joan of Arc.

4 Master of Baroncalli Portraits (fl. ca. 1480–90)
Saint Catherine of Bologna with Three Donors
Courtauld Institue of Art Gallery, London

Saint Catherine of Bologna (Catherine Vigri) enjoyed a humanistic education and was herself well versed in the art of manuscript illumination, of which many examples have survived. As here, she is commonly depicted with a book in her hands, a reference to her extensive mystical writings, in particular, the treatise *The Seven Spiritual Weapons,* first printed by Bolognese nuns in 1475 and frequently reprinted during the 1500s.

In Italy Saint Catherine of Bologna (Catherine Vigri, 1413–1463) gained public recognition through her religious treatises such as the *Treatise on the Seven Spiritual Weapons,* a guide to spiritual life. Printed by nuns in 1475, it was one of the earliest printed works in Bologna, and greatly admired by novices and female aristocratic readers. Catherine Vigri grew up at the court of Nicholas III d'Este, Marquis of Ferrara, where her father worked as a diplomat. In this environment, she enjoyed an exceptional humanist education and was also trained in the fine arts, especially

As long as books were a rare and almost unattainable commodity, reading was very much an aristocratic privilege.

the art of manuscript illumination. In 1456 she became mother superior of the Poor Clares Convent in Bologna, founded by Colette of Corbie, a Frenchwoman, some twenty years earlier. The convent still contains a breviary, *Pregare con le Immagini*, written and beautifully decorated by Catherine. A facsimile edition of this work is still in print. She also painted frescos, miniatures, and panel paintings, some of which have survived until today. She was canonized on 22 May 1712 and is the patron saint of artists.

As long as books were a rare and almost unattainable commodity, reading was still very much an aristocratic privilege. This was to change in 1454 with the invention of the printing press in Europe. It is of note that printing with moveable type had already been invented in China during the culturally advanced Song Dynasty (960–1279). Some 200 years before Johannes Gutenberg printed his famous Bible, the life's work of the poet Yi Kyu-bo (1168–1241) had been set in metal moveable type in Korea and printed on handmade mulberry paper. There is no indication, however, that the European invention by Gutenberg was not an independent one.

Martin Luther (1483–1546) was the first writer to use printing as a vehicle for the mass distribution of reforming and revolutionary ideas, intentionally reaching out to the entire population. His *Ninety-Five Theses* were in wide circulation between 1517 and 1519. Before that, printing pamphlets or papers for wider distribution had been done only by universities for their disputation manuscripts. The precursors to Gutenberg's revolutionary invention were block-books, in which—rather than using small interchangeable pieces of moveable type—letters and images were carved together into a single large woodblock and printed, one block per page. The printing of block-books began in Europe in the early fifteenth century before eventually being replaced by moveable type around 1480. In China, Japan, and Korea block-books had been in use since the eleventh century and remained in use longer than in Europe, since the great number of characters in these languages made printing with moveable type impractical.

As the printed word gained momentum, it became theoretically possible for even the poor to own and read books. In practice, however, most books—other than the Scriptures, some instructive literature, and poetry—remained out of reach for ordinary people, let alone women. Contemporary images showed book within contexts of piety and devotion. Paintings of the Annunciation, for example, frequently depicted Mary reading at the moment of the Archangel Gabriel's arrival to announce her being chosen to conceive the Holy Spirit (page 36). The presence of the book in these images not only stresses Mary' piety and virtue, but sometimes even serves as an example—in good medieval theological tradition—of how the Old Testament prefigures the New: Mary is traditionally depicted reading the passage from Isaiah 7:14 "Therefore the Lord himself will give you a sign. Behold a young woman (virgin) shall conceive and bear a son and shall call his name Immanuel." The book, in these images, always encompasses a number of symbolic meanings.

Pre-Renaissance images of women reading were often populated by legendary or saintly figures. In the following centuries, social, economic, and technological changes would profoundly affect the practice and culture of reading, and women's access to education and reading matter would grow. The paintings produced during these centuries vividly reflect many aspects of this new and expanded culture of reading by women. Art as well had evolved to include portraits of real women, mothers and daughters, mistresses, and wives. The rich variety of these images vividly shows the new social and cultural meanings the act of reading by women would come to assume.

The World's First Author

Disk of Enheduanna,
Akkadian, ca. 2300–2184 B.C.
Cuneiform inscription in Sumerian
University of Pennsylvania Museum of Archeology and Anthropology, Philadelphia

The Akkadian princess and high priestess Enheduanna is the world's first recorded author, having self-assuredly placed her name on her cuneiform tablets. Appointed by her father Sargon, the King of Akkad, to the prestigious office of high priestess and wife of the moon god Nanna, she was responsible for maintaining the Akkad dynasty's cult and for praising its wise rule. For this purpose, Sargon, also known as the "king of Kish," placed her at an important Sumerian center, in Ur, an area he seized control of in his expansionist politics of asserting full dominance over the Babylonian heartland. Enheduanna's literary works comprised temple hymns, poems, and incantations and remained of unmatched sophistication until the time of Sappho.

Carved in bas-relief, on one side the moon-shaped work depicts a ritual offering to the moon god Nanna by Enheduanna. The cuneiform inscription on the other side reads: "Enheduanna, zirru-priestess, wife of the god Nanna, daughter of Sargon, [king] of the world, in [the temple of the goddess Inan]na-ZA. ZA in [U]r, made a [soc]le (and) named it: 'dais, table of (the god) An'." The disk shows four distinct figures in relief taking part in an offering before an altar to the left. The dominant and best preserved figure, Enheduanna, is depicted in a flounced dress and wears an *aga*, or rolled turban. The composition has the "simplicity and elegance of a Greek 'theory' or sacred procession."

The Greek Poetess

Sappho or La Poetessa
Wall fresco, Pompeii, date unknown
National Archeological Museum, Naples

Possibly the greatest of all lyricists ever, Sappho's (fl. ca. 600 B.C.) passionate and erotic poetry—hymns to goddesses, love and wedding songs full of yearning—composed to be accompanied on the lyre, was meant to educate her female audience in all matters of the heart, grace, charm, and the arts. In Sappho's Greece women teachers devoted themselves to their promising young pupils, who eagerly followed their teachers and passed on their legacy. Sappho's inspiring work, of which some 200 fragments and one complete song remain, has fascinated readers throughout history. Not only the common man but also great philosophers fell under her spell (Plato, for example, elevated her to the status of tenth muse in anticipation of future generations' continuing admiration of her literary creations). Her reputation as one of the greatest poets of all time is still intact after 2,600 years. Even today, Sappho still exemplifies women's achievement in the arts and cultural refinement.

Historical texts provide little information about Sappho's life other than that she came from an aristocratic family and was married to Cercylas from the island of Andros, a wealthy tradesman and many years her senior. Myths about Sappho abound, such as that she had homoerotic inclinations, which, if so, were not uncommon in the Greek society of her times. The most unfounded legend, however, concerns her death, according to which she took her life by drowning herself at sea because of unrequited love to Phaon, a sailor and much younger man. The real circumstances and the year of her death are not known. Sappho has been the subject of artistic representation throughout history, from antiquity to the present. The fresco illustrated here portrays her in a pensive mode with a stylus and tablet.

The Roman Wife

Wife of Paquious Proculus, A.D. 79
Detail of a wall fresco, Pompeii
National Archaeological Museum, Naples

It is known from documentary sources that painted portraits were very popular in the Roman world, but due to the vulnerability of their locations only a few of them have survived; thus the preserved wall frescos in Pompeii are of outstanding importance. The fresco from which this detail is taken is from Pompeii, House VII, 2,6. It dates from the last years of Nero's reign, and is thought to be a portrait of Paquius Proculus (a magistrate) and his wife.

One of the few "public activities" of Roman women was the writing of poetry, although their work, independent of its quality, was generally not taken seriously by the very patriarchal Roman society. From her pose we can assume that Proculus's wife was a poet, since she is portrayed—just like the fresco of the so-called Sappho (page 24)—with a stylus and wax tablet, the usual attributes. Her hair is styled in the latest fashion of the day and her earrings with their pearl pendants were a symbol of her status. Roman women enjoyed a certain degree of education if only for the purpose of bringing up good sons, their most important duty. In this respect Roman as well as Greek women would be seen by later civilizations as model mothers.

虞帝舜
周太姜
周太任
周太姒
漢成帝
班倢伃者班彪姑也成帝初即位選入後宮

China's Great Woman Scholar

The Story of Ban Zhao
(A.D. 45–115)
Lacquer screen from
Sima Jinlong's tomb
Datong, China,
before A.D. 484

Detail
Ban Zhao's *Admonitions for Women* is the type of book written by a woman specifically for the woman reader. Its subtle phrasing indirectly taught elite women strategies for surviving intrigues at court and in the households of their husbands.

Canonized as "Chinas greatest female scholar" by the male intellectual circles of her time, Ban Zhao was the author of *Admonitions for Women*, or *Nüije,* a conduct book for women that would influence gender socialization from the Eastern Han onward. Carefully phrased in order to avoid posing any threat to masculine authority, the work emphasizes the importance of education for women, yet at the same time reasserts Confucian principles and values. In fact the author advised women to be submissive and self-sacrificing for their own good, yet newer interpretations of *Admonitions for Women* indeed suggest that the work reveals an "extremely sophisticated strategy teaching elite women" how to deal with and survive the obstacles they faced in their husbands' household and the life-threatening intrigues and plots at court long enough to eventually attain power themselves.

In her capacity as the first female historian, the versatile Ban Zhao compiled, edited, and completed the history of the Western Han dynasty, the *Han Shu,* which consisted of 120 volumes and was written by several members of her family in succession: The record was started by her historian father, who died when Ban Zhao was just eight years old and then continued largely by her brother Ban Gu, who was executed in A.D. 92 for political reasons. The emperor himself summoned Ban Zhao for this monumental task, which opened to her the treasures of archives and books in the Imperial Library. It took her some fourteen years to complete the history. The *Book of Han* remains an important work for Chinese scholars and the question of how much can indeed be credited to Zhao has been the subject of scholarly debate for 1,900 years.

The Pillow Book

Portrait of Sei Shonagon (968–ca. 1025) by Kikuchi Yosai from the woodblock book *Zenken Kojitsu*, 1868
Courtesy of C.V. Starr East Asian Library, Columbia University

Sei Shonagon entered court service around 990 as lady-in-waiting for the Empress Teishi (also called Sadako). She served her until 1000 when the empress died during childbirth at the age of twenty-four. Sei's fascination with the young empress and the elegant life at court inspired the *Pillow Book*, a collection of poetry and observations, and gossip, covering an entire decade of life at the refined Heian Court (784–1185) as well as intriguing poetic observation of nature.

Known for her wit, some of Sei's chapters bear titles such as "It Is So Stiflingly Hot" and "To Meet One's Lover." She also writes of boredom, a common experience for women in the court, since one of their main occupations was sitting behind screens looking pretty. But it was precisely this leisure-sickness that led to women's literary achievements. Faced with a limited choice of reading material, they began to take up writing themselves. The title *The Pillow Book* relates to the reader's habit of keeping this type of literature at her bedside or in the drawers of her wooden pillow, a form of private consumption that seems well captured in this portrait drawing of Sei Shonagon, who gazes out from behind a curtain, surrounded by books. The title could also refer to Sei's own account of an incident in which Sadako handed her a "bundle of notebooks," for which the empress had no use and Sei suggested, "Let me make them into a pillow." But it is uncertain whether this passage is authentic. *The Pillow Book* brought great fame to Sei Shonagon and is considered by many to be the best contemporary document of life at the sophisticated Heian Court. Little is known about Sei's private life; apparently she was divorced, had at least one daughter, and died lonely.

The artist, Kikuchi Yosai (1781–1878), son of a samurai, was famous for his monochrome portraits of historical figures, documented in his history of Japanese heroes, the *Zenken Kojitsu*, first printed as a woodblock book in 1836.

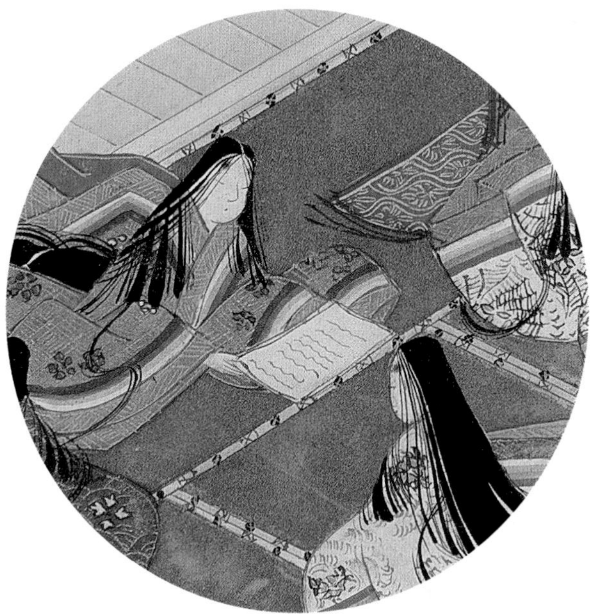

The World's First Novel

The Eastern Cottage
Scene from *The Tale of Genji*, Edo Period
Collection Mary Griggs Burke
Courtesy John Bigelow Taylor, New York

Murasaki Shikibu (ca. 973–ca. 1015) wrote the *Tale of Genji* in the Ishiyama Temple near the city of Ootsu, Shiga Prefecture. The room in which she worked is beautifully preserved and can still be seen there. The present painting illustrates chapter fifty, in which a lady-in-waiting reads aloud to a group of friends whom she has invited to her house with the aim of consoling one of them about an unhappy romance.

The Tale of Genji is generally considered the world's first novel and represents one of the great masterpieces of Japanese literature. Written some 1000 years ago, it is still in print today, often in exclusive and beautifully illustrated formats. The novel (consisting of 54 volumes of about 25,000 lines) is a complex tale of the life of the fictitious Prince Genji ("the shining prince") and his love for his various concubines. It is a beautiful and psychologically profound reflection of the duality of life at the colorful Heian Court, its splendor, its crimes and intrigues, and the anxieties, sorrows and pain hidden behind the visible lives of this unique society of aristocrats with its capitol at Heian-kyo, present-day Kyoto. It is this reflection that makes the tale so outstanding.

Lady Murasaki wrote at a time when Japanese culture was at a crossroads. Turning away from the traditional imitation of Chinese arts, Japanese writers and artists began to create their own indigenous style in literature, calligraphy, painting, and other fields. No other work of Japanese literature has inspired more—sometimes legendary—illustrations than *The Tale of Genji*. Scenes from the novel have been produced in a great variety of formats, media, styles, and techniques. The most celebrated are those from the Tosa School, of which the present scene is an example. The original, twelfth-century handscroll is now at the Tokugawa Museum.

Detail
A lady-in-waiting reads a passage from the *Tale of Genji* to her friend, hoping to console her about an unhappy romance.

The First Great Voice for Women's Education

Master of the *Cité des Dames*, ca. 1405
Illumination from the book *Cité des Dames* by Christine de Pizan
Bibliothèque Nationale de France, Paris

Detail
The allegorical figures Reason, Justice, and Rectitude guide Christine de Pizan's construction of a symbolic city of women.

In *The Book of the City of Ladies* and *The Book of Three Virtues*, both of 1405, Christine de Pizan (ca. 1363–ca. 1431) argues for and demonstrates women's intellectual capabilities, and vehemently defends them against ridicule. In an observation that would echo through subsequent centuries in various forms, de Pizan argued that if little girls were sent to school and taught the same subjects as boys, they would learn just as fully and would understand the subtleties of all the arts and sciences. For this reason among others, Christine de Pizan is regarded as the first voice to publicly advocate for the intellectual potential of her sex, the first "crusader for women's rights."

Born in Venice, de Pizan grew up comfortably at the French court where her father was the physician for Charles V. The first Western woman to support herself and her three children by writing, de Pizan wrote in the vernacular, a novelty in itself. Her texts revealed such a wide range of knowledge and understanding of her contemporary culture and society that they attracted attention in the highest circles; her patrons included the duke of Orleans, Queen Isabeau de Bavière, the Fourth Earl of Salisbury, and Philip the Bold of Burgundy. In this miniature from *The Book of the City of Ladies*, the three allegorical figures Reason, Justice, and Rectitude assist de Pizan in constructing a symbolic city of women, in which they can take refuge and defend themselves.

Cy commence le livre de la cite des dames duquel le premier chappitre parle pourquoy et par quel mouvement le dit livre fu fait .

Selonc la coustume ma
niere que iay en usaige
et a quoy est dispose le ex
cercice de ma vie cest assa
voir en la frequentacion
destude de lettres un jour comme je fusse seant
en ma celle avironnee de plusieurs volumes
de diverses matieres mon entendement a celle
heure aucques travaillie de recueillir la pesanteur
des sentences de divers aucteurs par moy lo
ngue piece estudiees dreçay mon visaige en sus
du livre deliberant pour celle fois laissier em
paix choses soubtilles et mesbatre et regarder
aucune joyeusete des dis des poetes et comme
adonc en celle entente je cerchasse entour moy
aucun petit livret entre mains me vint da
venture un livre estrange nonmie de mes
volumes qui avec autres livres mavoit
este baillie si comme en garde adonc ouvert
cellui et veu en sa titulacion que il se cla
moit matheolus lors en soubzriant pour
ce que oncques ne lavoie veu et mainte
fois oy dire que entre les autres li
vres cellui parloit bien a la reverence de
femmes me pensay que en maniere de so
las le visiteroie mais regarde ne lot gue
longuement quant je fus appellee de la bonne
mere qui me porta pour prendre la reffec
cion du souper dont leure estoit ja venue
proposant le veoir lendemain le
laissay a celle heure le matin ensuivant
rassise en mon estude si que iay de coustume
noubliay pas mettre a effect le vouloir
qui mestoit venu de visiter cellui livre
de matheole adonc pris a lire et proceder

The Divine Reader

Master of Flémalle
Robert Campin and workshop (South Netherlandish, Tournai, ca. 1375–1444)
Central panel of the Mérode Altarpiece, 1425–30
The Metropolitan Museum of Art, New York, The Cloisters Collection

The *Mérode Altarpiece* is one of the most famous, masterful, and widely studied Early Netherlandish paintings. In a novel departure from tradition, Campin places the Annunciation not in a church setting, but rather in a domestic interior containing a wealth of vividly portrayed details. Campin's obvious love of detail in the representation of objects of daily life would come to characterize Early Netherlandish painting, with its mixture of the sensuous and symbolic, presenting a wealth of symbols for the viewer to "read."

"The Archangel Gabriel arrives in the room followed by a tiny image of the Christ Child born on rays of light and carrying a cross. Their entrance appears to have extinguished the candle burning on the table, but the Virgin, absorbed in her reading with downcast eyes, seems momentarily unaware of her heavenly guests." The Virgin has a choice of reading material, and the book that lies open on the table, while carefully rendered to mimic the appearance of a fifteenth-century manuscript, is a simulation, not a recognizable text, although it is known from other contemporary representations that the Virgin is reading the Old Testament prophesy of a Virgin birth in Isaiah.

The Master of Flémalle was a painter from the Netherlands who got his name from three paintings in the Staedelsche Kunstinstitut in Frankfurt that were incorrectly believed to have come from Flémalle, near Liege. Scholarly opinion today is that the master is in fact Robert Campin (ca. 1375–1444), who was the leading artist in Tournai at the time.

The Wisdom of the Magdalene

Rogier van der Weyden
(ca. 1399–1464)
The Magdalen Reading,
before 1438
The National Gallery,
London

In the fifteenth century the printed word was still predominantly the realm of men and, with the exception of empresses, queens, and other high-ranking royalty, women depicted with a book were almost exclusively female saints. In addition to the Virgin Mary, the foremost divine reader, Mary Magdalene, was frequently portrayed with a book in hand, a reference to her wisdom.

In this fragment cut from an altarpiece of the Virgin and Saints, Mary Magdalene reads the "book of books," the Holy Scripture. Absorbed in her studies, she is oblivious to her surroundings. The jar in the foreground contains the ointment that the Magdalene rubbed onto Jesus' feet in repentance for her sins.

As in Campin's *Mérode Altarpiece*, here too, the figures are depicted in a contemporary domestic interior and the text of the book is simulated, only the gothic letters D and A can be identified.

One of the most important and influential Netherlandish painters of the fifteenth century, Rogier van der Weyden (ca. 1399–1464) is known for his highly personal and emotional style, which skillfully infuses the present painting as well. The *Magdalene Reading* is one of three remaining fragments (the other two being two small panels of Saint Catharine and Saint Joseph) from a larger panel of the Virgin with the infant Christ among saints.

The Virgin in Devotion

Antonello da Messina
(ca. 1430–1479)
Virgin Annunciate,
c. 1475–76
Galeria Regionale della
Sicilia, Palermo

In Christian iconography, blue is the color of the Virgin, the color of heavenly love, and the color of truth. This painting of the Virgin Mary, the divine reader, showing her behind a lectern with an open prayer book, is one of the most exquisite and mysterious of all fifteenth-century paintings. The Virgin looks up from her reading, not quite meeting the viewer's gaze, and raises one hand delicately from her page. The composition is of unmatched harmony and structural clarity and the hands have even been considered the most beautiful ever painted. "It has, without apology or exaggeration, been compared to Leonardo da Vinci's *Mona Lisa* (Musée du Louvre, Paris) and as with that painting, there is really nothing like it."

Trained in the Neapolitan workshop of Colantonio (a master steeped in the Netherlandish style), Antonello da Messina (ca. 1430–1479) was one of the most innovative and outstanding painters of the age of Humanism, and a genius of the Italian Renaissance. His portraits are extraordinary for their almost physical naturalism, for the quality of their light and the way it illuminates the surfaces of objects, and for the positioning of their figures. His style marked a new era in the development of portrait painting in Italy.

Words are Seeds

KOREAN PROVERB

Piety and Luxury: Women Reading in the Sixteenth through Eighteenth Centuries

In portraits of women reading from this period the sitters are now contemporary women and no longer exclusively saints or legendary figures. Produced for a variety of purposes, these images show women in many different social roles, including donors, mistresses, artists, women of leisure, and mothers. These paintings illuminate the various meanings the act of reading had for women, expressing attitudes of piety or frivolity, responsibility, or social status. The women depicted are still primarily members of the social elite. Their representations reflect the social and cultural functions of portraiture during these centuries and also mirror women's limited access to education and reading material in society as a whole.

In sixteenth-century portraiture women who were members of the high aristocracy or royalty were often depicted in a regal pose. Others were shown as cultured mistresses of noble households, surrounded by musical instruments, objects of art, or fruit; the use of grapes symbolized family ties, for example. Occasionally an animal was present, usually a little dog. Such objects alluded to the woman's social graces and her virtues, as well as domestic harmony. Some animals in these pictures had underlying erotic connotations. The ermine, for example, was a symbol of virginity, as legend had it that it would die of shame if its white fur were stained. The book present in such portraits was usually a Bible, prayer book, book of hours, or occasionally a small volume of poetry. This reflects the centrality of devotional texts in women's reading during this period. Women's lives were shaped, of course, by the religious and moral values of the day; only later would women be depicted reading for purely intellectual purposes.

3 Maerten van Heemskerck (1498–1573) Altarpiece, right panel, ca. 1540–43, detail

4 Francois Boucher (1703–1770) Portrait of Madame de Pompadour, ca. 1750, detail

The religious and ethical norms that dominated in Europe around 1500 can be seen in the austere portrait of Lady Margaret Beaufort reading in her book of hours (page 52). Lady Beaufort (1433–1509) was the mother of Henry VII, founder of the Tudor dynasty, her only child despite four marriages. Even for the mother of a king, Lady Margaret's level of education was exceptional for her time. Although she did not read Latin, she treasured her library of English and French books. A munificent benefactor of learning, Lady Margaret promoted the early English press and established readerships in divinity at the universities of Cambridge and Oxford. She also endowed a chantry with local school obligations at Wimborne, Dorset. This school was free and open to all social classes, and accepted girls as well. But the opportunity for schooling remained theoretical, for a girl from a rural community was rarely sent to school. The rate of illiteracy in England at the time was probably about ninety percent if not higher, and those few women who could read commanded only rudimentary skills. Even for aristocratic girls, a culture of reading did not exist. Rather, they were educated by their mothers or female relatives in the "domestic arts" such as needlepoint and spinning. Lady Margaret herself trained a number of girls in these particular skills.

Books remained a rare and expensive commodity. A library list of the noble household at Leeds Castle of Sir Henry Guildford and his wife Mary Wotton (page 54) numbered around sixty books in their possession. They are categorized by size (large, medium, and small) rather than by subject. This practice was based on the books' monetary value: The larger a book, the more expensive it was; it also reflected the inheritance law, according to which women could inherent only smaller and thus less valuable books, which they would later hand down to their daughters.

In the first half of the sixteenth century, both the emergence of Humanism and the Protestant Reformation changed England's educational landscape. The brilliant but ill-fated English humanist Sir Thomas More (1478–1535) was a strong advocate of classical education for the girls of the nobility, even training some, including his three daughters, himself. For these privileged girls only, the educational curriculum now included classical literature, philosophy, mathematics, astronomy, and even rhetoric. But the common girl remained faceless, and these kinds of educational opportunities were not available to her. Girls from poor families were expected to work already by the age of seven to contribute to the family income.

As a result of the Protestant Reformation schools once administered by the church (convents and monasteries) were closed, and replaced by schools privately funded by the rich merchant class, who had their children educated there. Progress towards a more liberal education for girls continued under the reign of Elisabeth I from 1558 to 1603; a number of towns saw the founding of boarding schools for girls where they were taught some spelling and reading, music and needlework: a very different curriculum, of course, from that of their aristocratic contemporaries.

According to *Chaste, Silent and Obedient* (Suzanne Hull, 1982), between 1475 and 1572 only twenty-four books were directed at a female readership, amounting to one book every four years. In the following decade nineteen such publications appeared on the English book market. These books were mainly devotional works, housewifery manuals, and matrimonial conduct books. Women, however, read not only books published explicitly for them, but also other titles to which they had access, such as ballads and poems. The restriction and control of women's reading activity sometimes took curious forms indeed. In 1543 Henry VIII issued a decree forbidding women to read the Bible by themselves and requiring their husbands' supervision. Although withdrawn in 1547, this act reveals how contemporary society saw women's reading as potentially dangerous and in need of masculine supervision, and exemplifies the importance society placed on controlling women's reading. With the reign of King James I (r. 1603–1625) the progress of women's education experienced a serious reversal of fortune. King James was of the opinion that it was sufficient for a woman to be able to read and write her name. Consequently, he did not even educate his own daughter.

In contrast to the pious Lady Margaret, a half-century later the Italian aristocrat Laura Battiferri (1523–158?) is depicted reading poetry (page 60). Battiferri was not a queen by birth but, judging from her portrait of around 1555–60 by Agnolo Bronzino, she must have had the regal bearing of one. The portrait is considered one of the most compelling of the Italian Renaissance. Its fine rich colors and the sitter's posture of impenetrable reserve give her the air of a high priestess. A poet herself, Battiferi displays a book of sonnets by the great Renaissance poet and humanist Francesco Petrarch. The so-called Petrarchino with its refined literary language and themes of unattainable love, longing, and desperation was widely read by aristocratic women, for whom it obtained a cult-like status. Equally popular were the sonnets of Vittoria Colonna (1492–1547), the greatest female lyricist of the Italian Renaissance.

The enlightened attitude in Italian aristocratic circles enabled a number of talented young women to flourish.

Her *Rime de la divina Vittoria Colonna Marchese di Pescara* continued the Petrarchian literary tradition. Published in 1538, it quickly became a classic.

Open-mindedness about women's position in Italian society began to develop in the sixteenth century, particularly in the highly cultured and wealthy Italian city-states such as Florence, Venice, Milan, and Bologna. Humanistically-educated circles—the aristocracy and the rich merchant class—witnessed a virtual "women's renaissance," influenced by Baldassare Castiglione's widely-read *Il Cortegiano* (1528). This work advocated a humanist education for girls of noble background and the curriculum even included instruction in drawing and painting. But the *Cortegiano* was foremost a code of conduct, concerned with the "courtly etiquette"—dignity, kindness, humility, and grace—that a woman should display in the company of men. In contrast, the daughters of average townsmen and peasants had almost no opportunity for formal education. Their training was limited to household duties, and such skills could be learned at home. But even for many girls from the nobility the only opportunity for true scholarly pursuit remained the convents, the ultimate guardians of female education. Only when a common girl showed exceptionally promising talent would a convent education be accessible to her.

The enlightened attitude in Italian aristocratic circles enabled a number of talented young women to flourish. Sofonisba Anguissola (ca. 1535–1625) emerged as the first recognized woman painter of the Renaissance. The prerequisite for her success was an education that her parents, Amilcare Anguissola and his wife Bianca Ponzoni provided for her. The couple decided to educate their six daughters no differently than boys, even sending Sofonisba and her younger sister Elena to serve as apprentices in the workshop of Bernardino Campi, thus training them to become professional artists. This was highly unusual; indeed, an almost revolutionary act, for it was taken for granted that girls of noble backgrounds would never work. Painting in a workshop, as the word implies, is work. At the beginning of their apprenticeships, the girls were near the tender age of ten.

The status of the Anguissolas, an august aristocratic family in Cremona, made such an educational experiment possible. For most of society, this kind of training of women would have been too progressive. This explains in part why Sofonisba limited herself to the genre of portrait painting, which at the time was considered beneath the other genres and therefore did not pose a direct threat or challenge to her male colleagues, neither artistically nor commercially. Her father's ambition to make Sofonisba a famous artist was not only a result of his enlightened views. Her success was also pursued with an eye to the family's honor and social status. (Elena would eventually choose to join a convent, still considered to be the most noble "career" for a girl.) A patrician merchant involved in various ventures, including the book trade, Amilcare Anguissola succeeded in using his social network to bring Sofonisba's talent to the attention of Michelangelo. There are records stating that prior to her departure for Spain Sofonisba resided in Rome for two years to train with the great master. Michelangelo encouraged her artistic development, for example, by assigning her the difficult task of drawing a crying boy. This resulted in one of her most important drawings: *Girl and a Boy Who Was Bitten by a Crab*, which she later gave to the aging Michelangelo as an expression of gratitude for his support.

While modest in character, Sofonisba was a confident and determined woman whose talent brought her fame and admiration within the highest circles. In 1559 Philip III invited her to paint at his court in Madrid where the beautiful Sofonisba arrived in great style with an entourage of eight persons. Arriving in January 1560, she remained there until 1579. Sofonisba has the distinction of being the first woman painter to work abroad. As a role model and forerunner of women's advancement, Sofonisba's greatest achievement was that she clearly paved the way for the women artists who followed. She made the vocation of artist and painter socially acceptable for women. In her self-portrait of 1554 (page 58) she presents herself unadorned and pointing to her name on the open page of the book she holds, delivering a clear message. She not only hints at education being of the utmost importance but compellingly summons women to follow her path of knowledge and learning.

Sofonisba generally limited herself to the genre of portrait painting since large historical and mythological works were considered to be the province of men. It would be the resolute and strong-willed Lavinia Fontana (1552–1614) who would simply disregard this tradition. Trained by her father, the successful painter Prospero Fontana, Lavinia became the first European woman to pursue a full-fledged career as an artist. She received important commissions not only for portraits but also for monumental paintings of religious and mythological subjects such as *Anbetung der Hirten* of 1570–75, now in the Pinacoteca Communale Imola, or the altar painting for San Paolo fuori le Mura in Rome. Successfully painting subject matter that had previously been the exclusive preserve of male artists represented a great personal triumph.

Apart from Fontana working in a wider variety of genres, there was another important difference between Lavinia Fontana and Sofonisba Anguissola. Sofonisba's paintings had not been for sale, but were given as strategically placed gifts in high places with an eye to possible return favors. Her status made it impossible for her to sell a "product." Furthermore, her lifelong pension from the Spanish king afforded her economic independence in any case. Lavinia Fontana, in contrast, was the sole supporter of her family. She sold her works for high prices, which were paid willingly. Her husband Gian Paolo Zappi, a nobleman but minor artist, was soon relegated to the position of assistant, priming her canvases and managing the ever-growing household—Lavinia had eleven children. This modern marital arrangement was highly unusual in the sixteenth century.

By the end of the sixteenth century, a group of remarkably gifted and determined women had made substantial contributions to the culture of the Italian Renaissance. Apart from their brilliant performances in their own métier, the painters Sofonisba Anguissola, Lavinia Fontana, and Artemesia Gentileschi, the poets Vittoria Colonna and Gaspara Stampa, and the authors Lucretia Marinella and Moderata Fonte to name a few, took active sides in the "querelles des femmes," or gender debates. These women humanists pioneered women's intellectual and professional progress; they regularly corresponded and exchanged views with the period's most outstanding literati, and their reading list included the most refined literature of their day. But on the other hand, for women as for men, the Italian Renaissance was a "stage" for the high aristocracy and the wealthy to display their refined knowledge and cultural tastes. The circle of these wealthy women humanists was a tightly knit group, and not much of their learning or opportunity trickled down to the common woman. The discrepancy in educational standards between well-born and ordinary women remained grave. Even the lower nobility in the country neglected their daughter's education.

Around the 1640s, constant technological improvements led to the unprecedented expansion of book printing throughout Europe, and resulted in the publication of works by many authors who might otherwise have remained unknown. This could be argued even for Shakespeare, as well as for the Greek and Latin classics that were now being printed in the vernacular. As a result, an impressively diverse selection of books not only became available but also more affordable. The seventeenth century saw the highest increase in "female literature" explicitly catering to the early modern woman reader. The bulk of these works were still devotional books and practical and instructive guides. The shift towards easing access restrictions took place against strong constraints, but by the late seventeenth century a readership of women was firmly in place. A literate woman from a gentry household might have had access to travel narratives, a geography book, poems, belles-lettres and plays, and to some prose fiction and other light literature. Play and poems often saw several editions.

Some historians consider the so-called reading revolution to have started in the seventeenth-century Netherlands. The Dutch tradition of tolerance and liberalism attracted intellectuals, writers, and scientists from all over Europe who brought with them manuscripts that might have faced censorship in their home countries. Within this open climate, the city of Leyden became the center of book printing; half of the world's book production during the seventeenth century came out of their presses. Forty percent of all printed titles were devotional texts—the Bible was the bestseller. Travel books, adventure stories of seafarers, atlases, and scientific and intellectual books were probably intended primarily for men. In keeping with their egalitarian tradition, the Dutch sent their daughters to school. The most important subject on the curriculum was reading, not least due to the fact that Protestantism, often called the religion of the book, decreed that every person had to be able to read the Bible. (For the same reason, in 1642 the New England colonies also introduced a law stipulating full literacy.) Writing skills, however, did not receive the same attention. The neglect of writing instruction was common; in late sixteenth-century France, for example, girls where explicitly forbidden to learn to write. In contrast, a century later, in England and America, a command of fine handwriting became an essential sign of refinement and sophistication for a young lady. The Protestant Reformation significantly increased literacy and educational standards. As a result, the average woman in northern Europe was a more active reader than her sister in the still conservative Catholic south.

1 Jean Francois de Troy (1679–1752)
La lecture de Molière, ca. 1730
Private collection

The image represents the Salon culture established by affluent and powerful women in France; the poet Molière is reading to a group of ladies from his own works.

While the list of accomplished seventeenth-century painters is long, it is Vermeer who has given us the most poetic and exquisite paintings of women. We see women of affluent households reading or writing a letter, instructing the maid, and often clad in glowing transparent colors and adorned in his famously lustrous pearl earrings. Vermeer does not portray women reading books but engaged in the more intimate activity of reading a letter, which was frequently connected with romance in the Dutch painting tradition. In only two paintings does Vermeer prominently include a book next to a woman as part of his visual vocabulary. One is the *Allegory of Faith* (page 74), reflecting the seventeenth-century context in which women's increasing literacy was principally intended to strengthen faith, a woman's most important virtue. In *The Art of Painting* of around 1666–67 (Kunsthistorisches Museum, Vienna) the book symbolizes history, and the woman displaying the book is its muse Clio.

The idea of a woman pursuing an intellectual education for its own sake was still seen as utterly foreign, if not outright absurd. When the *wunderkind* Anna Maria van Schurman (1607–1678)—who could already read and translate Latin texts at the age of seven, and would eventually be proficient in twelve languages—became the first woman invited to attend the University of Utrecht in 1636, she had to sit behind a curtain and remain invisible to the all-male student body. Van Schurman, the first woman ever to graduate with a degree in law, was probably the most highly educated women of her time. It is no surprise that she questioned women's role in society. In her book *Whether the Study of Letters is fitting for a Christian Woman* of 1646, she strongly advocated for women's education in all subjects as long as it did not interfere with their domestic duties.

As the Enlightenment began to transform France in the eighteenth century, the bourgeoisie became the new driving force in society. But these changes in societal structures did not bring about much improvement for the lower classes. The education of the common girl was generally no better than that of her mother, rudimentary and limited to household duties.

In the higher echelons of society this was the era of the Salons, ruled by wealthy or aristocratic women. Every new book was greeted with enthusiasm and even ecstatic or hysterical tears. The exuberant "feminine Rococo" became the style of luxurious and intimate interiors, imbued with soft colors and charming effects. These interiors (often works of art in their own right) not only housed delightful small sculptures and lovely porcelain but also provided the ideal setting for reading. The Rococo reader was often a "frivolous" consumer rather than an earnest scholar. Reading had become a favorite pastime for women of means. In a society devoted to material comfort, special furniture was designed to improve the pleasure of reading, such as the elegant chaise longue and other special chairs. (This trend can be dated as far back as the fourteenth century, and older documents attest to the crafting of special reading desks and other devices.) Despite the general liberties and frivolities of the era, as well as the fact that it was fashionable for women of status to read, reading by women remained an activity viewed with a certain amount of suspicion. In contrast, the desire to own and admire paintings

2 Sir Thomas Lawrence
(1769–1830)
Mrs. Jens Wolff, 1803–15
The Art Institute of Chicago

Mrs. Wolff is studying a book of Michelangelo's engravings in the pose of the Erythraean Sibyl from the Sistine Chapel ceiling. The sitter separated from her husband, the Danish Consul, in London in 1810. Lawrence was deeply in love with Mrs. Wolff and the intense interest he displayed in the son she had around this time led to the suspicion that he was the father.

was considered harmless. It was believed that a picture only showed what was visible, but that a book could always contain some hidden and possibly dangerous message.

Paintings from the eighteenth century depict women gracefully reclining on their luxurious furniture in their even more luxurious costumes (page 78). They are smiling, dreaming, contemplating, and thoroughly enjoying themselves while deeply immersed in their books. Indeed, one could argue that these paintings reflect the widely feared seductiveness of reading. As in earlier periods, secular books in a woman's portrait were not an indication of intellectual pursuits but contributed to the overall sensuality of the image and were often intended to flatter the sitter's delicate sensibilities. The symbol of a non-religious book in a person's portrait was easily defined: For men it represented power and knowledge; for women, luxury or refinement.

The culture of reading for women was not only one of sensuous luxury and aristocratic leisure. Different social groups had different aims. In England, newspapers had become established by the second half of the seventeenth century. The first was the *London Gazette* in 1666, with the *Ladies Mercury* being founded in 1693. Papers such as the *Tatler* (1709), *Spectator* (1711), and *Guardian* (1713) had readers of both sexes. Women writers, however, and particularly women journalists were in a precarious position in a predominantly male literary culture. Their attempts to bring their messages of dissent against the poor state of women's education and status in society across to the woman reader could have dire consequences. Mary de la Riviere Manley (1663–1724), the author of the notable and controversial *Secret Memoirs from the New Atlantis*, founded the *Female Tatler* in 1709. Her articles rebelling against the political and social order were branded downright scandalous, and she was promptly thrown in jail. Women had no business expressing opinions on matters of public interest. After her release, her colleague Jonathan Swift (1667–1745) whose masterpiece *Gulliver's Travels* (1726) had raised many eyebrows, made de la Riviere editor of *The Examiner* newspaper. Again, she became the target of constant defamation and libel suits. Eventually she conceded that reading and writing about politics and other matters of public life were not the business of women and from then on composed harmless stories suitable for a "female" readership. Anne Dodd, a news-seller and pamphlet shopkeeper, became editor of the *London Journal* in 1721. She faced the same persecution in 1728, and was only released from prison by faking an illness.

Women journalists in France did not fare much better, yet political developments encouraged them to unite and to challenge the establishment. (The number of growing feminist societies was remarkable.) Newspapers such as *La Gazette des Halles* and *La Gazette de la Place Maubert* were widely circulated. Articles arguing for women's rights in general as well as their increased access to knowledge were written by women and like-minded men and aimed at a "female revolution." Women activists—one could call them "femmes fatales du parole"—took to the streets of Paris reading to the illiterate and most oppressed women of the time, such as peasants, washerwomen, and prostitutes. The *Journal des Dames*, published from 1759 to 1778, was so militantly feminist that it scared away even progressive and open-minded female readers.

Despite revolutionary developments, women's educational and professional advancement left much to be desired. Even the most privileged and talented of women had to resort to lobbying to overcome barriers to their progress. The highly successful and celebrated Paris painter Élisabeth Vigée-Le Brun (1755–1842) needed to be a protégé of someone in power in order to achieve her ambitious

Women activists took to the streets of Paris reading to the illiterate and most oppressed women of the time.

goal of becoming a member of the Académie Royale, an almost entirely male institution. She found her patron in her personal friend Queen Marie Antoinette, of whom she painted some twenty portraits. With the change of political circumstances her association with Marie Antoinette forced her to leave France to seek work in various courts throughout Europe, from Russia to England, Italy, and Austria. For Vigée-Le Brun a nomadic life, and a lonely one at that, began. Yet her reputation always preceded her, and her exceptional talent secured her commissions for painting the royalty at all these courts. Although living among the rich and famous, Vigée-Le Brun's private life was overshadowed by tragedy. She was exploited first by a greedy stepfather who squandered her hard-earned money and then later by her fortune-hunting husband who practically ruined her.

An unfortunate choice of husband was also the fate of her contemporary, the Swiss-born painter Angelica Kauffmann (1741–1807). Although Vigée-Le Brun outdid her in portraiture, Kauffmann was equally talented and the two are regarded as the most respected female artists of the eighteenth century. Angelica Kauffmann, like Vigée-Le Brun, learned her craft from her father. Along with painting, her great passion was reading and she sought out the company of writers and historians wherever she lived, leading to an intimate friendship with Johann Wolfgang von Goethe, whom she met in Rome in November 1786. Goethe became her "personal reader," sharing from his own writings with her during their "very personal recreational hours," and Kauffmann translated some of his stories onto her canvases.

Book printing continued to expand, but women writers still constituted a minority of the great authors who appeared on the book market during the eighteenth century. Printing and reading practices reflected society's ideas of gender and gender roles. Children's literature, which arrived on the growing book market around 1740, was no exception: fairytales and domestic stories for girls, adventure yarns for boys. But girls also felt the need to satisfy their adventurous spirits, and it comes as no surprise that they clandestinely raided their brothers' bookshelves.

One reason for the small number of printed works by women writers was the lack of willing publishers, even in the case of the great Jane Austen. When she first presented the manuscript of *Sense and Sensibility* for publication the publisher refused to even look at it. *Sense and Sensibility* (1795) and *Pride and Prejudice* (1797) were finally published anonymously at the author's own expense in November 1811, the year in which she wrote *Mansfield Park*. At least included was the remark that they were written "by a lady." Praised as masterful, her novels received excellent reviews and enjoyed a wide readership among women. The congenial Austen became an established author, yet her real identity remained unknown to the general public until it was posthumously revealed by her brother in 1817.

As for the educational system of her time, Jane Austen's description of an upscale school run by the Misses Stevensons in London in her book *Emma* as "a seminary, or an establishment or anything which professed, in long sentences or refined nonsense, to combine liberal acquirements with elegant morality upon new principles and new systems—and where young ladies for enormous pay might be screwed out of health and into vanity" clearly expresses her verdict on the quality of contemporary education. Also known as the "ladies' Eton," the seminary had a minimal academic curriculum like any other school at the time and its "prime object was to instill Decorum, Manners and Deportment."

Some decades later, aware of the prejudices against female authors, the Bronte sisters submitted their manuscripts under the "noms de plume" of Currer (for Charlotte, 1816–1855), Ellis (for Emily, 1818–1848), and Acton (for Anne 1820–1849) Bell. After a painful search for a publisher, their novels caused a great sensation, as did the revelation of their true authorship. *Jane Eyre* (1846), for example, initially received critical acclaim and was celebrated in literary circles until it was revealed that the author was a woman. The tone changed immediately, and the work's language was condemned as shockingly coarse, offensive, and downright scandalous. Literary magazines warned female readers not to read it. The vitriol went so far as to accuse Charlotte of being a sex-starved careerist, and to claim that Emily had lovers of both sexes. But the intense outrage and the personal accusations accompanying their publication could not prevent the novels by the "three spinsters from a moorish land" from becoming bestsellers.

From the close of the Middle Ages through the Rococo, representations of women reading were associated either with piety (page 52) or seduction (page 80) or with the particular roles of mother and teacher (pages 62, 82); examples of women reading for culture and edification emerged as well (pages 60, 64). But as women artists and writers overturned barriers and opened up new professional possibilities and educational opportunities, by the end of the eighteenth century, new kinds of images emerged which arguably show women reading as an intellectual pursuit (pages 90, 114). This new culture of reading stands in stark contrast to the Rococo images of sensuality and luxury associated with women's reading as well as the pious attitudes of reading for edification or religious instruction. While a true democratization of reading remained distant, in the next century increasing numbers of women were taught to read, and the reading material itself continued to grow in diversity. Reading by women could assume a much richer variety of cultural meanings and social roles, all of which are visible in the images that depict them.

The Book of Hours

Rowland Lockey
(c. 1566–1616)
Lady Margaret Beaufort
(1443–1509), ca. 1597
St. John's College,
Cambridge

Lady Margaret Beaufort (Countess of Richmond) kneels devoutly with her hands raised in prayer. The book of hours open before her is large and exquisitely produced, as befits the mother of a king. Books of hours possessed by common people, if they had one at all, were much smaller. The book of hours is an abbreviated breviary containing texts for each liturgical hour of the day. Over time, books of hours came to include calendars of the religious and secular year and prayers to local saints as well.

The splendid interior of Lady Margaret's "private closet" or prayer room behind her chamber forms a stark contrast to her austere attire (a nun's habit). Mother of Henry VII, founder of the Tudor Dynasty, and a woman of great piety and learning, her charitable endeavors were dedicated almost exclusively to education and learning. She founded Christ's and St. John's Colleges in Cambridge as well as the Lady Margaret's professorships of divinity at Cambridge and Oxford. Oxford's first women's college, Lady Margaret Hall, founded in 1878, was named in her honor.

Rowland's painting is a copy of an unidentified earlier work, presumably of around 1500. The portrait was presented to the college by Julius Clippersby in 1597. The following entry about the mounting of this painting in the chapel appears in the college rentals for the third quarter of 1597:

"To two carpenters for settinge upp the foundresse picture xvid
For fyve pillers in the creste of the Chappell border & for makinge a newe
creste for the newe picture of the foundresse vs
For gildinge & payntinge the crest over the foundresse picture xiiis."

ANNO M·D·XXVII ÆTATIS·SVÆ·XXVII

Tudor Splendor

Hans Holbein the Younger
(1497/8–1543)
Mary, Lady Guildford, 1527
Saint Louis Art Museum

The prayer book in the hands of Lady Guildford is inscribed with the title *Vita Christi*, identifying it as an edition of Ludolph of Saxony's (d. 1378) highly popular Life of Christ, used as a devotional text in England as throughout Europe. Lady Guildford (b. 1500) was the second wife of Sir Henry Guildford, comptroller of the royal household, member of the royal order of the Garter, and a favorite of Henry VIII. Sir Henry (1489–1542) commissioned the present painting and a pendant of himself by Holbein, now at the Royal Collection in Windsor.

Sir Guildford is sumptuously attired in gold, and shown with the attributes of worldly power and success—he holds a white staff and wears the collar and badge of Saint George—while Lady Guildford's attributes are symbols of piety and devotion such as the small leather-bound book and the red rosary beads to count prayers. The tiny sprig of rosemary tucked into her bodice symbolizes remembrance and may refer to the immortality the sitter has attained through Holbein's brush. Her portrait, however, speaks equally emphatically of the Guildford's secular splendor. Her sleeves of gold cloth, the six gold chains across her bodice, the rings and gold necklace with pendant, the exquisite gold-tasseled bookmark, and the pearls that frame her extravagant headdress in typical Tudor gable fashion complete the image of unbounded opulence.

Both Guildford portraits were executed during Holbein's first visit to England. The artist later returned to England in 1532 and within four years became court painter to Henry VIII. In this capacity he painted four of the king's six wives in succession, not without risk: Holbein earned the king's wrath, for example, for his overly flattering representation of Anne of Cleves.

Family Prayer

Maerten van Heemskerck
(1498–1573)
Altarpiece, right panel,
ca. 1540–43
Kunsthistorisches Museum,
Vienna

Detail
In alter triptychs, the devotional book before the woman is documentary evidence of women's roles as caretakers of their families' spiritual values.

In the late Middle Ages and early modern period, it was common practice for wealthy families to commission altar triptychs for private worship at home or for the parish church. The central panel of these triptychs was always a religious scene (in the present it was a lamentation). The depiction on the left and right panels varied and often showed the donor and his wife, as in this altarpiece, in which the left panel portrays the male members and the right panel the female members of the patron's family. The coat of arms at the lower left seems to be that of the van Uitwyck family of Brabant.

The female members kneel piously before a prie dieu. The donor's wife gazes out at the viewer, with her daughters kneeling behind her, whereas the elderly, black-hooded woman is most likely her mother or mother-in-law. In almost all depictions of this kind, it is the woman rather than her husband who is shown with a devotional book, a reference to her as a good, quiet, and contemplative wife, occupied with the spiritual welfare of her family and in particular its female members. The book here symbolizes the donor's piety but also helps to mediate her relationship to the scene of the lamentation depicted in the central panel. Like the rosary she holds, both book and painting were instruments of religious practice and often, as in this case, worked together to mutually reinforce the practitioner's devotions.

Heemskerck intensified his "Italian style" during his stay in Rome from 1532 to 1535. Many northern European artists traveled to Italy in the sixteenth century to study the art of their contemporaries in the South. The inspiration they derived from this experience resulted in the introduction of new elements into their religious paintings, which became more worldly than the inward-looking art of the fifteenth century.

Sophonisba
Angussola
virgo.
seipsam
fecit
1554

The First Renaissance Woman Painter

Sofonisba Anguissola
(ca. 1535–1625)
Self-Portrait, 1554
Kunsthistorisches Museum, Vienna

Detail
By pointing to her name on the open page of the book, Sofonisba literally summons women to follow her path of knowledge and learning.

In this unadorned self-portrait, Sofonisba Anguissola's open book communicates a clear message: she presents herself neither as aristocrat nor artist but as a young humanistically-educated woman. She gazes steadfastly out of the image space as if inviting her fellow women to follow her path of education, knowledge, and virtue, for the words on the open page read "Sophonisba Angusola virgo seipsam fecit 1554." In referring to herself as "virgo" the artist associates herself with the famous woman painter Iaia (later called Marcia) of antiquity, who chose to remain chaste in order to concentrate fully on her art. Sofonisba later abandoned her identification with Iaia. She married first in 1572 and, after her first husband's untimely death, a second time in 1579, and apparently led a very fulfilling life both personally and as an artist.

The gifted Sofonisba was only nineteen when she painted this tiny self-portrait but already at the age of fifteen she had been registered in the Olymp *Inter egregious pictores nostri temporis* by the famous Cremona bishop and humanist Marco Gerolamo Vida. This self-portrait may have been a present by Cardinal Alessandro d'Este to the Austrian emperor Rudolf II. Born into an august aristocratic family in Cremona and trained by the masters Campi and Gatti, Sofonisba became the first acclaimed woman painter, an achievement made possible by a new open-mindedness towards women's position in society that developed in the great age of Humanism in Italy's aristocratic circles. Sofonisba's success literally paved the way for the women artists who followed. She made the profession of artist socially acceptable for women.

Exquisite Poetry

Agnolo Bronzino
(1503–1572)
Laura Battiferri, ca. 1555–60
Palazzo Vecchio, Florence

In this Renaissance portrait, Laura Battiferri's exquisite gesture displays a book of sonnets by the humanist Francesco Petrarch (1304–1374), addressed to her namesake "Laura" (Laura Noves was the mysterious love of Petrarch). The book she shows the viewer is not accidental. It attempts to place her firmly within the Petrarchian poetic tradition and holds his work up, so to speak, as the model to which women should aspire. Indeed the sitter, Laura Battiferri (1523–158?) was herself a distinguished poet and her literary creations were read and admired by women and men in her intellectual circles, to which such prominent writers as Toquato Tasso and artists such as Benevenuto Cellini belonged. Her poetry also attracted keen readers at the court in Spain, who had her work translated into Spanish.

A renowned portraitist for the Medici court, the great Florentine painter Agnolo Bronzino subtly captures the elusive grace of his sitter's character, which was thought to have been an incarnation of devotion and chaste and noble beauty. Her elegant but austere dress reflects the rigid Catholic norms of her time; the veil was a standard attribute of married women and an allusion to chastity. Battiferri's second husband, whom she married when she was twenty-seven, was the distinguished architect and sculpture Bartolomeo Ammananti.

Mother and Tutor

Lavinia Fontana (1552–1614)
Widow and her Daughter,
1592–1595
Pinacoteca Nazionale,
Bologna

The portrait of mother and daughter joined by a small prayer book clearly implies that shared reading, recitation, and prayer played a central role in the education, handed down, as it were, from mother to daughter. The image depicts an ideal aristocratic maternal relationship within a clearly defined social world, framed by the cultural climate of late sixteenth-century Bologna. The noblewoman, a widow, is depicted in accordance with her society's expectations of her as both mother and tutor of her daughter. The elegant and yet austere costumes—both figures are dressed in black with strings of black pearls around their necks—emphasize the mother's status as widow. The entire composition is an intentional expression of the seriousness of the mother's role as protector and teacher of her daughter, and her duty of raising her to be a good Christian. This is further seen in the protective gesture of the mother's arm around her daughter's shoulder. The sitters of the painting have not been identified. The arrangement of the two figures recalls paintings of Saint Anne teaching the Virgin to read.

Born in Bologna, Lavinia Fontana was the daughter of the painter Prospero Fontana, who trained her in the art of drawing, thereby laying a solid foundation for her craft (she later apprenticed with Denis Calvaert). Unlike Sofonisba Anguissola, Lavinia was the first women painter to sell her works, which included important commissions for religious and mythological paintings as well as portraits. At the age of twenty-five she married the artist Paolo Zappi, who was of higher noble lineage than Lavinia, but without an inheritance. Nor was he much of a painter. By mutual agreement the husband took over the management of their large household, including its finances. All income was generated by Lavinia, who was frequently pregnant (she had eleven children), and theirs was a modern marital arrangement, highly unusual at the time.

Devotional Reading

Gerard Dou (1613–1675)
Old Woman Reading
a Bible, ca. 1630
Stichting Het Rijksmuseum, Amsterdam

Detail
The illustration in the open page of the Bible shows Simon, the tax collector, watching Jesus' arrival while perched in a tree; Jesus looks up at him.

The old woman is reading a passage about Jesus' arrival in Jericho, an episode from the Gospel according to Luke. She holds the book up close, studying the illustration intently. Both her face and the page are brightly illuminated and rendered in close detail. The illustration in the large volume shows Simon, the tax collector, who watches Jesus' arrival from a tree he has climbed, while Jesus looks up at him.

Initially trained as an engraver and glass-painter, Gerard Dou joined Rembrandt's workshop as an apprentice in 1628 for about three years. He soon developed his own style and became a master at representing his subjects by candlelight. After Rembrandt left Leyden for Amsterdam in 1631, Dou was the city's leading artist, although he never attained the fame of his master. His oeuvre comprises some 200 paintings. The present painting is also known as "Rembrandt's Mother."

Leyden was a city of intellectual freedom and the center of book printing in the seventeenth century. Literacy was fairly widespread and women enjoyed a basic education. At the time this picture was executed, however, their reading activities were still largely limited to religious texts. In the following decades a wider range of literature would become available to women, such as plays, poetry, and prose fiction, sometimes published in expensive quarto editions of 500 exempla.

The Traveling Saint

Francisco de Zurbaràn (1598–1664)
Saint Margaret of Antioch, 1630–40
The National Gallery, London

Dressed in the picturesque costume of a shepherdess and with the features of a contemporary woman there is nothing otherworldly about Zurbaràn's Saint Margaret. With an air of decisiveness and determination—saddlebag over her arm, book in hand—she seems on her way to spread the Word. The dragon accompanies her almost protectively. In deeply Catholic Spain reading and reciting devotional texts remained more central to women's literacy for longer than was the case in the North. One of the great Spanish painters of his time, Zurbaràn was also deeply pious and his images reflect his personal—and the national—piety more than those of his contemporaries such as Velázquez and Murillo.

According to legend, Margaret declared herself a Christian virgin and refused to "marry the prefect of Antioch. She was thereupon thrown into a dungeon where she was devoured by Satan in the form of a dragon." But the dragon freed and "delivered" her by bursting open. The virgin martyr of fourth-century Antioch consequently became the patron saint of pregnant women and of childbirth.

Born into a family of minor merchants, Francisco de Zurbaràn was repeatedly assisted by his friend Diego Velázquez in obtaining public commissions such as the decoration of the royal palace in Madrid, Buen Retiro with the series *The Labors of Hercules* of 1624. Zurbaràn is best known for his mystical and spiritual paintings, but there is also an exceptional beauty to his still lifes. Pious women and saints were among his favorite subjects. Most of his paintings of female saints—such as twenty-four canvases of virgin saints for Lima and fifteen for Buenos Aires—were commissions, and his series were largely executed by assistants. The painting of Saint Margaret of Antioch, however, is not part of such a series but clearly an autograph work.

The Educated Regentesses

Johannes Cornelisz Verspronck (1601/03–1662)
The Regentesses of the St. Elisabeth Hospital in Haarlem, 1641
Frans Hals Museum, Haarlem

Detail
The regentess invites inspection of her official records.

This painting was commissioned by the regentesses to adorn their office and shows them in a meeting with an open cash book on the table. They are apparently discussing the finances of the St. Elisabeth Hospital, for which they were responsible. The woman on the right holds out her open hand, a gesture presumably indicating "that their records are open to inspection and that the regentesses are accountable for their action." The hospital's executive body comprised four female regents and five male regents, of whom Frans Hals (1580/5–1666) painted a picture in the same year. Verspronck renders his regentesses with rosy and friendly-looking faces in stark contrast to the frightening-looking *Lady-Governors of the Old Men's Almhouse in Haarlem*, painted by Frans Hals in 1664 and also in the Frans Hals Museum.

The women who served as regentesses of charitable institutions such as hospitals or almshouses, and who ran them as honorary bodies, were usually well educated and of aristocratic background, or from the town's leading families. Such hospitals cared for the poor and needy, who were given free medical treatment and food for a period of six weeks. Located near such hospital were often poorhouses and workhouses for "fallen girls." In these greatly feared institutions, which housed mainly poor girls and orphans, inmates worked under often grueling conditions "in return for a mere pittance." The girls were most likely illiterate with no prospects of even the most basic education. The workhouse next to the St. Elisabeth Hospital, and partly financed by it, also served as a prison and mental asylum, and was a grim place indeed.

To Read and Sew

Georges de La Tour
(1593–1652)
The Education of the Virgin,
ca. 1650
The Frick Collection,
New York

Detail
The education of the Virgin served throughout history as an example for raising devout daughters.

The subject of the education of the Virgin first appears in fifteenth-century books of hours and generally shows Mary reading from a Bible held by her mother Saint Anne. In these images, Mary is depicted as both the well-educated girl and virgin; later, in depictions of the Annunciation, she will become the divine reader. According to apocryphal sources, Mary was well trained by her mother, who also taught her to read and sew. In the seventeenth century, education for girls included the domestic arts, but also solid knowledge of the alphabet, as can be seen in the needlework samplers produced at the time. Learning to read and sew were intrinsically linked, almost a Biblical inheritance. The education of the Virgin served as an example for mothers in raising devout daughters.

There are numerous elaborate treatments of the Virgin's education by such masters as Tiepolo, Murillo, Delacroix, and Rossetti, among many others. Georges de La Tour was a native of Lorraine and spent most of his life there. His style appears to have been influenced by Caravaggio and his Dutch followers. Like the present work, his later religious paintings are often nighttime scenes very tender in feeling, lit by a single candle as light source.

Morally Uplifting Literature

Eglon van der Neer
(1635/36–1703)
The Reader, ca. 1654–64
The Metropolitan Museum of Art, New York

The woman is most likely engrossed in one of the morally uplifting books by the Dutch poet Jacob Cats (1577–1660). Cats' writing was permeated with Christian norms and values and was especially popular among less well-educated women. His emblem books enriched with poems enjoyed a particularly devoted readership among women centuries after his death.

"Whether the woman pauses in her reading in order to reflect or because she has been interrupted is difficult to say." The "interrupted reader" was already a well-established motif, as for example in Titian's 1548 portrait of the *Empress Isabella* (Prado, Madrid) or Anthony van Dyck's *Portrait of a Woman, Called the Marchesa Durazzo* of 1621–27 (Metropolitan Museum of Art, New York). Central to these representations is the idea that the figure is absorbed in thought, suggesting a certain degree of intellectual cultivation. Whereas the books in Titian's and van Dyck's painting are religious, in the present painting the woman is reading a secular book. The writing set with the piece of sealing wax is another sign of literacy.

Born in Amsterdam as son of the landscape painter Aert van der Neer, Eglon van der Neer was an accomplished painter of genre scenes and classical landscapes, but also found his place as a portraitist. Two of his paintings of 1665 are closely related to the present one, *Woman Seated at a Table with a Book and a Mirror* and *Young Woman with a Plate of Oysters*, the latter now in the collection of the Liechtenstein Museum in Vienna.

Faith, Light, and Iconography

Johannes Vermeer
(1632–1675)
Allegory of Faith,
ca. 1670–72
The Metropolitan Museum
of Art, New York

Detail
Counter-Reformation Catholics also placed newfound emphasis on education and the Bible. The hand on her breast indicates that faith lives in the figure's heart.

The exquisitely rich *Allegory of Faith* centers on the figure of a woman in a white and blue satin dress. She is surrounded by attributes and instruments of faith: a painting of the crucifixion behind her, a cornerstone that has crushed the snake, and an apple as a reminder of original sin. The presence of the book here is also allegorical: The prominent place of the open Bible emphasizes the Word, juxtaposed with Christ's body (the crucifixion) and blood (the chalice), as an indispensable element of faith. Vermeer derived most of the components of this allegory from the Italian writer Cesare Ripa's (ca. 1555–1622) *Iconologia*, an iconographic handbook of mythological and allegorical figures in which Faith is the most important virtue. The book was translated into Dutch in 1644.

The son of two reformed Protestants, Vermeer converted to Catholicism before his marriage to Catherine Bolnes in 1653, which almost certainly affected the choice of subject in his historical paintings. This picture was probably executed for a private Catholic patron or for a "hidden" Catholic church. Vermeer's works are unsurpassed at representing the effects of light, for which he used a number of mechanical and painterly means, for example, the *camera obscura*, mirrors, and different textures of paint to intensify his visual effects.

Cultural Refinement

Thomas Gainsborough
(1727–1788)
Portrait of a Woman,
ca. 1750
Yale Center for British Art,
Paul Mellon Collection

In the early eighteenth century a diverse selection of readily available printed materials—magazines, newspapers, and books (in particular poetry and innocent and innocuous novels)—helped to create a culture of reading. In portraiture of the time, the figure of a girl with a book offers a reflection of women's more prevalent and diverse reading activity. These images generally do not yet depict reading as an intellectual activity, however, but are rather intended to suggest the emotional sensitivity, imagination, and personal virtue of the sitter. The book is clearly an object of leisure and cultural refinement in Gainsborough's painting. The sitter's resemblance to the 1750 painting of *Miss Lloyd* (Kimbell Art Museum, Texas), has led scholars to conjecture that she is a member of the famous Lloyd family of Ipswich, but this identification has not been firmly established.

Together with Sir Joshua Reynolds, Thomas Gainsborough was the most sought-after portraitist in England, and even Europe at the time. He was a painter with a particularly sharp eye for the specific characteristics and beauty of his sitters.

Patron of Arts and Luxury

Francois Boucher
(1703–1770)
Portrait of Madame de Pompadour, 1756
Alte Pinakothek, Munich

Madame de Pompadour (1721–1764), the most famous mistress of the French king Louis XV, had a personal library of thousands of volumes and was a great patron of the arts and literature. In this capacity she supported, for example, the philosopher and writer Denis Diderot (1713–1784) in his controversial project of the *Encyclopédie, ou dictionnaire raisonné des sciences, des art et des métiers*, systematic dictionary of the sciences, arts, and crafts, comprising thirty-five volumes and published between 1751 and 1780. The intellectual impact of the *Encyclopédie* is thought to have shaped the civil and literary history of its century.

However, de Pompadour, the daughter of a Parisian merchant, was also an incarnation of luxury, and her reading material might have included the genre known as "libertine literature," such as Cleland's *Fanny Hill, The Memoirs of a Women of Pleasure* of 1748–49, or the great stage plays of Molière, Racine, and Beaumarchais. Her library also included Voltaire's philosophical novel *Zadig* (1747) and *Candide* (1759), as well as the early works of Rousseau.

Francois Boucher was a great admirer of Madame de Pompadour and has pictured her comfortably stretched out on what seems to be a chaise longue in typical Rococo Salon fashion. It was painted while she was lady-in-waiting to the Queen. Here as elsewhere, the artist is unmatched in his reflection of the spirit of his day: elegant, frivolous, sensuous, and to a certain extent, artificial.

Erotic Literature

Francois Boucher
(1703–1770)
Resting Girl
(Louise O'Murphy), 1751
Wallraf-Richartz-Museum,
Cologne

Extravagant frivol paintings, like the present work in which the figure suggests an air of conspiracy, were popular among collectors during the Rococo era. "No less than the legendary Giacomo Casanova (1725–1798) writes in his memoirs that the sitter for this painting was the fourteen-year-old Louise O'Murphy, and that Boucher sold it to the brother of the Marquise de Pompadour, the Marquis D'Argenson, Foreign Minister" at the time. Apparently it was by means of this painting that the girl's beauty was brought to the attention of King Louis XV who took her as one of his mistresses in 1753. Having given birth to the king's illegitimate daughter (Agathe Louise de Saint Antoine, 1754–1774) the young O'Murphy became increasingly ambitious and tried, naturally in vain, to assert herself against the powerful Madame de Pompadour. But Madame de Pompadour's mastery of the intrigues of court politics was unsurpassed, and she had O'Murphy married off without delay to Jacques de Beaufranchet, a lesser nobleman.

Marie-Louise O'Murphy (1737–1814) was the daughter of an Irish army officer who immigrated to France and set up shop as a shoemaker in Rouen. After his death, the mother brought her five daughters to Paris, where Marie-Louis apparently initially worked as a seamstress, but started modeling for Boucher in 1751. The painting reflects the Rococo era's luxury, frivolity, and sensuality—including reading, as indicated by the book on the footstool near the sofa. Perhaps O'Murphy is reading the erotic novel *Les Bijoux indiscrets* (*The Indiscreet Jewels*) of 1748 by Denis Diderot, or Pierre Carlet de Marivaux's successful stage play *Le Jeu de l'amour et du hazard* (*The Game of Love and Its Dangers*) of 1730. A nearly identical painting of O'Murphy by Francois Boucher is at the Alte Pinakothek in Munich, albeit without the book.

Reciting the Gospel

Jean-Siméon Chardin
(1699–1779)
The Good Education,
ca. 1753
Museum of Fine Arts,
Houston

A young child taught by her mother or governess was a favorite subject of Chardin's. In the present painting the woman puts aside her embroidery to devote her full attention to the girl who—as likely understood by eighteenth-century viewers—is reciting a passage from the Gospels. Scholars have pointed out the relationship between *The Good Education* and works such as Francois Fénelon's *De L'education des filles* (1693), an educational tract that remained influential in Chardin's day. One passage reads: "It is necessary to prevail upon young ladies to read the gospel. Accordingly, select for them a good time of the day to read the word of God . . . Above all, inspire young girls with that sober and restrained wisdom which Saint Paul commends." A painting of a similar subject by Chardin now in the National Gallery in London, *The Young Schoolmistress*, from around 1735–36, was engraved in 1740 by Lepiciè with the following inscription: "If this charming child takes on so well the serious air and imposing manner of a schoolmistress, may one not think that pretence and artfulness come to the fair sex no later than birth."

Known for his subtle compositions and sensitive interpretations, Chardin delighted in recording his subjects' emotions: The girl is obviously worried, perhaps about a lapse in her recitation. The mother, who has put down her embroidery, shows concern, yet looks at her daughter tenderly. The entire composition radiates warmth and tender feeling. Chardin's domestic genre paintings with scenes from the everyday life of the middle classes (women taking tea, governesses, washerwomen, weary travelers) project a humanity, domesticity, and veracity that are greatly admired today. During his lifetime, however, it was his still lifes of animals, birds, and fruit that earned him the greatest fame.

DE NEWTON

Gravity and Airs

Maurice Quentin de La Tour (1704–1788)
Mme. Ferrand Meditating on Newton, 1753
Alte Pinakothek, Munich

The Enlightenment brought enormous social changes to France, and wealthy women—like the sitter, who came from a family of influential magistrates—had access to an almost limitless variety of literature. Mme. Ferrand's morning activity, meditating over Newton rather than dressing up and being concerned with her make-up, makes clear claims to the sitter's intellectual interests. On the other hand, La Tour was known for his talent of flattering his sitters' intelligence, and these claims can, therefore not be taken entirely at face value.

The painting certainly reflects the rise of a highly educated bourgeoisie. The reading activity here could thus be more of an affectation, constructing a fiction of intellectual pursuit in order to underscore the sitter's membership in a specific social class. The average woman rarely had access to books, let alone scientific books. Neither did she have the financial resources or the time to indulge in the "idle activity" of reading.

Born in Saint-Quentin, Aisne, Maurice Quentin de La Tour was a master of pastels, and an exhibition of several paintings from a series—eventually numbering 150 splendid portraits—at the Paris Salon in 1737 was talked about for decades afterwards.

The Reluctant Reader

Sir Joshua Reynolds
(1723–1792)
Gertrude, Duchess
of Bedford, 1756
By kind permission of His
Grace the Duke of Bedford
and the Trustees of the
Bedford Estates

The proud and high-spirited Gertrude, Duchess of Bedford, more than once found herself the object of pointed comments in various contemporary writing. The scandalous *Whig Club* of 1794 referred to her as "a stingy and avaricious woman" and some contemporaries described her as "very stately in her drawing room, though at other times very condescending" and as someone who will "go to anybody that will give her cards or supper" and "the most artful and dangerous of women."

Despite being somewhat unpopular, Gertrude was loved by her children and had a marriage based on mutual devotion. Her pose and pensive, even dissatisfied, look, however, could lead one to imagine that she has just read precisely such an unflattering comment about herself. But the open pages of her book are not legible, and the real subject of her reading activity remains the object of speculation.

Sir Joshua Reynolds was a founding member of London's Royal Academy and its first president as well as the author of the influential *Discourses on Art* (1769–1790). Reynolds was renowned for his sure sense of what was appropriate to a sitter's age and social and political position. Very few paintings of women reading can be found in Reynolds vast oeuvre, which would indicate that the reading activities of his female sitters were not of particular interest to him.

Gertrude Dutchess of Bedford
wife to John Duke of Bedford

A Civil War Novel

Angelica Kauffmann
(1741–1807)
Louisa Hammond, ca. 1780
Fitzwilliam Museum, Cambridge

The sitter, Louisa Hammond, features in Samuel Jackson Pratt's novel *Emma Corbett or, The Miseries of Civil War founded on some Recent Circumstances which happened in America*, Dublin, 1780. The novel, about the American Revolution and its impact on private lives, "recounts the love of Henry Hammond for Emma Corbett and that of his sister, Louisa Hammond for Emma's brother, and is written in the form of letters exchanged between the various characters. Kauffmann's painting illustrates Letter XXXIV." Samuel Pratt (1749–1814) was a prolific British writer of novels, travel narratives, and stories for juvenile readers, and a contributor to literary magazines. An ex-actor and clergyman, he published under various pseudonyms.

Angelica Kauffmann had moved to London in 1766 and as a founding member of the Royal Academy she participated in the academy's annual exhibitions between 1769 and 1782. Her career soon reached its first zenith, securing her a remarkable income, which, however, her fortune-hunting husband, Count the Horn squandered. This ill-fated marriage weighed heavily on her. In 1781 she married the artist Antonio Zucchi, and they moved back to Rome the same year. There, in November 1786, she met Johann Wolfgang von Goethe, with whom she cultivated an intense friendship, leading to a bitter-sweet romance. While in her company, Goethe endlessly admired her accomplishments, yet back in Weimar, he would criticize her "feminization of painting," claiming that her works lacked passion and expressiveness and that her portraits of men were devoid of dignity and masculinity. Art history, however, has not concurred with Goethe's evaluation. Precisely those qualities condemned by Goethe have come to be seen as the artist's most significant contribution to portraiture: her ability to "civilize" her sitters and bring out their most noble traits. Indeed, she is said to have "virtuously cultivated" her male patrons. Hers was a culture of sensibility.

An Educational Volume

Élisabeth-Louise Vigée-Le Brun (1755–1842)
Portrait of Mrs. Chinnery, 1803
Indiana University Art Museum

Leaning against a velvet cushion, Mrs. William Chinnery reads a book by the French writer and educator, Comtesse de Genlis. It might be *Mademoiselle Clermont* of 1802, de Genlis' greatest romance, but considering the size of the volume it is most likely one of her educational works. De Genlis (1746–1830) also wrote historical novels, which were much admired in England for their "purist style."

Vigée-Le Brun, who received her first instruction from her father, the pastel painter Louis Vigée, arrived in England in 1803 where Mrs. Chinnery, a popular hostess of London's high society, became one of her very few friends (Vigée-Le Brun never really warmed up to the country or its people). In pre-revolutionary Paris, Vigée-Le Brun, renowned also for her exceptional beauty and compelling character, had maintained a highly sought-after Salon frequented by the intellectual and artistic elite, including the unyielding journalist, playwright, and staunch feminist Olympe de Gouges (1748–1793, born Marie Gouze), who wrote the *Declaration des Droits de la Femme* in 1791 and was publicly guillotined on 3 November 1793 for being a "reactionary."

During these political upheavals, Vigée-Le Brun was denounced for her close association with Marie Antoinette as well as for her outspokenness on questions of gender; she fled Paris on the eve of 6 October 1789. For the divorced Vigée-Le Brun and her nine-year-old daughter Julie, an unstable and nomadic life began. They lived in nearly every European capitol and she worked at nearly every court, in particular those in Russia and England.

The veil Mrs. Chinnery is wearing was a headdress fancied in the Regency period. It evoked a sense of medieval Europe, giving its wearer the feeling of a heroine stepping out of a Gothic novel, a favorite genre of literature at the time.

The Minister's Daughter

Thomas Pole
(1753–ca. 1829),
attributed to
A View through the
Window into the Garden
with a Lady Writing,
14 St. James' Square, 1806
Bristol Museums,
Galleries & Archives

Detail
Historically minister fathers were often unusually supportive of their daughter's studies.

The young woman sits studiously at a desk, intently concentrating on her writing and surrounded by books, some of which are obviously for immediate reference, as the open pages suggest. The library, crowded with bookshelves and overlooking the garden, is in the house of Dr. Thomas Pole, a physician and Quaker minister. Pole's was a learned household that obviously encouraged his daughters' intellectual and academic interests, an attitude still uncommon in the early years of the nineteenth century, even among genteel young women. The sitter is probably one of Pole's daughters, either Eliza or Rachel. Her white dress with square scarf and bonnet were typical indoor daywear.

Historical records have shown that ministers were often unusually supportive of their daughters' intellectual curiosity, rather than seeing it as grounds for anxiety or irritation. This was even more true of Thomas Pole, who seems to have been involved in pioneering reforms in adult education in Britain.

This painting belongs to a series of seven charming, if naïve, watercolors with meticulous attention to the details of St. James' Square. With the exception of the present one, all the watercolors in this series depict Pole's impressive and historically important (late Georgian) urban garden. Next to his other occupations, Pole was an accomplished gardener and also an amateur painter; the watercolors are probably his work.

The Neglected Education of My Fellow-Creatures Is the Grand Source of the Misery I Deplore.

MARY WOLLSTONECRAFT, A VINDICATION OF THE RIGHTS OF WOMAN

Connecting with Books: The Nineteenth Century

Paintings of women reading in the nineteenth century, and in particular its second half, depict different kinds of sitters than the pious or aristocratic patron who dominated earlier images. Representations that displayed the book primarily as an attribute of its owner's privileged status and access to knowledge or as a comment on her moral character have been replaced by less formal images of the artists' family members and friends, professional models, or simply neighborhood people. Women reading are now depicted in a variety of contexts: in the privacy of their own homes, in the lush environment of gardens, in public places, or artists' studios. Artists found inspiration and material for individual and cultural definition in familiar people, places, and patterns of behavior. Although these paintings are still expressions of reading and education as something refined and elevated, they now shift their focus to the individuality of the women they depict, and books have become symbols of interests outside the domestic sphere and its duties. Reading comes to symbolize the world of the imagination. These new images of women reading interpret and reflect on modern life and focus on the world of experience. They also presuppose economic and social changes: greater tolerance for women reading, a loosening of restrictions, and access to a greater variety of literature. They depict reading primarily as a subjective experience; the nature of the books themselves is now secondary.

On the other side of the Atlantic, in the American colonies, as in Europe, women's reading material in the seventeenth century consisted primarily of scripture; the education of girls was informal and took place at home. A true explosion of formal and eventually more equal education for girls occurred only a century later, accompanying the cannons of the American Revolution in the eighteenth century, when it was realized that not only the manual but also the intellectual abilities of women would be essential to build the fledgling nation.

Anne Bradstreet and Mary Rowlandson were among the first writers to write so-called colonial literature. The unusually well-educated Anne Bradstreet (1612–1672) came to the Massachusetts Bay Colony from England. Her book *The Tenth Muse Lately Sprung Up into America* (1650) was the first published work by an American woman. These mostly religious poems, deeply embedded in Puritan life and its strict moral code, comforted her women readers in dealing with the hardships of daily life. Mary Rowlandson's (ca. 1637–1710/11) powerful account of her and her three children's captivity by Indians in February of 1676 was a bestseller on both sides of the Atlantic. The story's strong religious message was, of course, part of its success and secured it a devoted female readership. *A Narrative of the Captivity and Restoration of Mrs. Mary Rowlandson* ran through more than thirty editions after its first publication in Boston in 1682.

Printing had arrived in the American colonies with the pilgrims. The first printing press was established in Cambridge in the Massachusetts Bay Colony in 1638. Operated by Stephen Day, its first publication was the *Bay Psalm Book* in 1640; as in Europe, early American publications were chiefly of religious texts. Most reading material still came from England in those days, and one popular eighteenth-century periodical in the American colonies was the *Female Spectator* from London. The paper was run briefly (1744–46) by the prolific writer and occasional actress Eliza Haywood (1693–1756). Haywood not only wrote some seventy works, including fiction, drama, poetry, and conduct literature, but was also active in politics throughout her life and was an important voice in periodical literature. One of her foremost causes was to mobilize mothers to fight for their daughters' right to an education. Elite women read her tracts with enthusiasm.

Demands for the improvement of women's education were continuously voiced by the young nation's leading women such as Abigail Adams, Eliza Pinckney, and Annis Boudinot Stockton. The educational background of these women themselves was actually quite varied. Eliza Pinckney, for example, was schooled in England (at Mrs. Boddicott's school for upper-class girls) and her studies included Latin, a knowledge she passed on to her daughters. Many other girls, despite being from wealthier families, had little formal education; educational responsibilities for girls rested mainly with their families and was not considered an obligation of the state. Massachusetts law, for example, stipulated that every town had to operate a public school, but these were for boys only. In the best circumstances girls were allowed to attend classes before or after the boys. In general, girls' education was rudimentary and often ended at the age of seven or eight. Their training consisted of cooking, sewing, sufficient literacy to read the Bible and prayer books, and a little arithmetic to cope with household chores. Poor parents trained their girls (and boys) for whatever work was likely to earn them some money to add to the family income. Even if the parents could read and write there was little time to pass these skills on to their children. In wealthier households, girls received additional training in the finer things of life such as music (piano and singing lessons), perhaps a little French, and social etiquette, for which outside tutors were hired.

Because of the lack of a formal system of education, Abigail Adams' father, the Reverent William Smith, himself supervised the education of his daughter and instilled in her a great passion for books. She read virtually everything in her father's excellent library, from Shakespeare, Pope, Milton, and Samuel Richardson to history books and legal texts.

Her keen interest was not necessarily a delight to her mother, Mrs. Elizabeth Quincy, who considered reading a waste of time. In the course of her studies, Abigail Adams (1744–1818) became one of the best-read girls of her time and would eventually become one of the most influential women in the country. Because of her own experience, she remained conscious of the lack of a formal education for girls and became a fierce advocate for it. In one of her famous letters to her husband she wrote, "you need not to be told how much female education is neglected nor how fashionable it has been to ridicule female learning." She also regularly corresponded on this matter with the prominent English historian and staunch Republican Catherine Macaulay and of course her dear friend the historian Mercy Otis Warren, author of the influential three-volume *History of the Rise, Progress and Termination of the American Revolution* of 1805, the first history book by a woman published in America.

1 Gilbert Stuart (1755–1828)
Matilda Stoughton de Jáudenes, 1794
The Metropolitan Museum of Art, New York

Matilda Stoughton de Jáudenes depicted in material splendor, was the wife of the Spanish chargé d'affaires to the United States. The painting shows her at the age of sixteen, just around the time of her marriage. Matilda's reading matter could be informational works about the country she was going to represent with her husband. Stuart, one of the most significant portraitists in American art history, demonstrates his more flamboyant style in this work.

These women increased public awareness of women's issues through their correspondence, and influenced the course of educational developments. It is significant that the most respected women writers at the time were historians rather than writers of poetry or romances; readers seemed to have less taste for poetry in the exciting times of nation building.

The first African-American woman poet of note in the colonies was Phillis Wheatley. Her book *Poems on Various Subjects, Religious and Moral* reflected her religious and classical New England upbringing and was successfully published in London in 1773. An engraving on the cover shows her composing (page 108). Phillis was brought to the New World on a slave ship from West Africa. Too young to be sold onto a plantation in the West Indies or the southern colonies, she arrived at the Boston slave market in 1761 at the age of around seven or eight years. There she was purchased by John Wheatley as a servant for his wife. Under the tutelage of the Wheatleys' eighteen-year-old daughter Mary, Phillis became proficient in English by the age of ten. She read the Bible regularly and began studying Latin texts as well as the poetry of Alexander Pope, in both of which she found much of the inspiration for her own writings. But although her unusual situation afforded her rare opportunities, and she was eventually given her freedom, Phillis' life was still determined by the social structures of slavery. Her life changed dramatically for the worse when three of the Wheatleys died within two years. Phillis continued to write poetry, but without the backing of a sponsor she could not find a publisher in America willing to take the commercial risk of publishing her work. She died in extreme poverty.

In the arts, the genre of portraiture flourished during the pre- and post-revolutionary period. Books are now found regularly in women's portraits, reflecting broader social developments, and they are meant to signify diligent study, educational responsibility, or philosophical contemplation and cultivation. Charles Willson Peale's *Mrs. Samuel Mifflin Instructing her Granddaughter Rebecca* (page 110) mirrors the practice of teaching girls at home, and the title of the book displayed, *Emblems, for the Entertainment and Improvement of Youth (1735)*, is self-explanatory. Ralph Earl's painting of Esther Boardman (page 112) is a classic attempt to communicate the sitter's emotional sensitivities and cultured background by means of a portrait. The elegantly dressed young Esther sits outdoors in a sylvan landscape, holding a small open volume of poetry, an expression of cultivation and sensibility, but less of knowledge. Knowledge as an attribute of the sitter was reserved for her brother's portrait: Painted at the same time by Earl, it depicts Elijah Boardman in front of his collection of books.

Despite the pioneering spirit of the young American nation and its generally encouraging attitude towards cultivating women's intellectual abilities, the belief remained widespread that men and women had separate tasks to fulfill and that the line between them should not be crossed. The main literary staples for women were primarily instructive and housewifery manuals, novels with strongly Puritan values, and religious and devotional texts, which were supposed to be studied daily. But because it was believed that history books and biographies also furthered moral improvement, women now slowly began to have access to these genres of literature as well.

As in Europe, in the young republic too, reading generally remained an activity of the upper classes; social gatherings (these were different from the literary clubs that were strictly a male domain) in which women discussed classical literature became popular, modeled after English and French examples. Women were now expected, indeed almost obliged, to participate in these discussions politely and gracefully, but of course not too cleverly. (Thomas More's opinion of some 300 years earlier, that a women should not show off her knowledge, was still firmly in place). To brave the conversation tables at tea parties and other fashionable events ladies armed themselves with a knowledge of classical literature and kept meticulous lists of the books they had read, exchanging these lists among themselves, annotated with comments. Their favorite books were such classics as Charles Rollin's *Ancient History*, Alexander Pope's *Iliad* (1715–20) and *Odyssey* (1725–26), and *The Adventures of Telemachus* (1699) by the French bishop and author François Fènelon. They read them in French or English translations, for knowledge of the classical languages (Greek and Latin) was still rare (and not necessarily desirable) among women. These heroic stories were particularly popular with women in part because of their confirmation of Puritan values, but also because the impeccable reputation and moral credentials of their authors could not lead to any objections on the part of their husbands, who still largely controlled their wives' reading activities.

Around 1800 half of Anglo-American women demonstrated alphabetic literacy, which, however, does not imply that they could read comprehensively. Calls for better educational opportunities were now frequently published in American magazines such as the *Massachusetts Magazine*, the *New York Mercury*, and the *American Museum*. As a result, when Mary Wollstonecraft's *A Vindication of the Rights of Woman* reached America it fell on fertile soil. Published in London in 1792, the treatise was received by the public with great interest, and enjoyed such a keen readership that booksellers could not restock it fast enough; it had to be reprinted in three more editions within a year, two of them for America. Unlike other advocates of women's improvement, Mary Wollstonecraft (1759–1797) not only argued that the educational system was degrading to women's faculties, she boldly called for an end to the gender hierarchy. Her opponents branded her demands utopian, and a decade after her death, with the change of political climate, her manifesto was even called an evil paper. Responses at the time ranged from the amusing to the nasty. The English writer Horace Walpole, the Fourth Earl of Oxford (1717–1797) called her a "hyena in petticoats," and her husband, the celebrated author William Godwin, referred to her "Amazonian temper." Some founding fathers denounced her as a "tub-thumper." Though not in full agreement with all of her ideas, Abigail Adams said they made sense to her, and Aaron Burr remarked to his wife, "you may have an advocate for your causes in this woman."

Mary Wollstonecraft was a radical and brilliant thinker, far ahead of her time; her *Vindication* was a truly revolutionary work, shocking to many of her contemporaries. Never has another woman philosopher's advocacy of women's potential been so profound and all-encompassing, with the possible exception of Simon de Beauvoir nearly 150 years later. Although Wollstonecraft's ideas were kept alive by women's rights movements, it would be some 100 years until policy makers considered her work seriously; only since the 1970s has she received true recognition for her achievements.

Wollstonecraft's early writings on women's issues, such as *Thoughts on the Education of Daughters* of 1786 or *The Female Reader* of 1789, did not yet reveal the full power of her mind but were conduct books written by a woman for women. At the time she ran a school for disadvantaged girls she had founded in 1784 in Newington Green (north London), which closed in 1786 for financial reasons. A subsequent position as a governess in Ireland lasted barely a year, and upon her return to London, she teamed up with Joseph Johnson, one of the most important publishers in England between 1770 and 1810. Johnson printed as economically as possible to make his publications affordable to a middle-class readership. Focusing at first primarily on popular religious works, in the 1770s and 1780s Johnson expanded his publishing to children's literature and philosophical works, and was one of the very few to publish women writers. Through Johnson Mary Wollstonecraft befriended leading thinkers of the French Revolution who further fired her already brilliant ideas. At the time she had become romantically involved (although some historians claim it was a platonic relationship) with the Swiss painter Henry Fuseli (1741–1825), a provocative interpreter of famous literary texts such as Chaucer's *Canterbury Tales* and Shakespeare. The relationship was painful and, despite Fuseli being a rebel himself, soured for several reasons (for one thing, Fuseli was already married to someone else), including her manifesto, with which he disagreed.

"Of the two-hundred-odd works of fiction produced by Americans between 1779 and 1829 better than a third were written for or by women."

Many enlightened readers thought differently though, and Wollstonecraft enjoyed great prestige in intellectual circles in England, France, and America; her ideas were widely discussed by men and women alike. It was her unconventional personal life, insensitively revealed posthumously by her surviving husband William Godwin in *The Memoirs of the Author of the Vindication of the Rights of Women*, that tainted her reputation and with it her achievements. Her first daughter Fanny was born out of wedlock because her American father, Gilbert Imlay, walked out on Wollstonecraft. She attempted suicide twice during this unhappy relationship. Her marriage bond with Godwin was sealed just days before the birth of her second daughter, the future Mary Wollstonecraft Shelley (1797–1851), author of the Gothic horror novel *Frankenstein*.

Mary Shelley's *Frankenstein* of 1818 is considered by many to be the first science fiction novel. The book's first edition appeared anonymously in 500 copies (the norm of the day) and in three volumes (the so-called triple-decker format of nineteenth-century first editions), but its author was soon revealed. Negative criticism about the absurdity and horror of the novel and warnings to the woman reader were quickly overshadowed by its readers' thrill, and it enjoyed a wide readership despite the criticism. Scenes that appear to be taken directly from Fuseli's famous painting *Nightmare* can be found throughout the book like an echo of her mother's unhappy affair. The story's future impact was enormous, laying the foundations for the genre of horror stories as well as for horror and science fiction films.

The well-educated and bookish Mary Shelley followed directly in her mother's footsteps, demonstrating an intellectual keenness and an almost militant free spirit from early on. At the age of seventeen she eloped with the equally non-conformist thinker and writer (and then still married) Percy Bysshe Shelley (1792–1822). The couple were friends with similarly free-spirited characters such as Lord Byron; stories of triangular love-affairs abounded. But however carefree and wild her youth may have been, Mary's life was haunted by tragedy. She suffered from feelings of guilt about her mother's death from childbirth eleven days after Shelly was born. Her half-sister Fanny Imlay committed suicide in October of 1816, followed by her husband's first wife in December. By 1822, at the age of twenty-five, Mary had been pregnant five times, of which only one child survived, and in July of that year, her (much philandering) husband drowned during a sea voyage at the age of twenty-nine. All told, it should be no wonder that she resorted to science fiction.

In keeping with the young American republic's claims for equality and democratic structures and its belief in the importance of educated citizens, the primary public role assigned to women was that of teacher, leading to the establishment of an ever growing number of "ladies' academies" all over the country. Great patrons, including John Adams, were won for these projects, and even the conservative Martha Washington took pride in the fact that her granddaughters would now have the opportunity for a formal education, although educational curricula for boys and girls were far from equal.

Institutions for educating girls flourished, such as Emma Willard's Troy Academy (est. 1814), Catherine Beecher's Hartford Female Seminary (est. 1823), or Mary Lyon's Mount Holyoke Female Seminary (est. 1837). The Winnsboro Female Institute in South Carolina, established in 1840 by Catherine Stratton Ladd, an art and education writer, soon had an enrolment of some one hundred pupils. Sarah Pierce's School for Young Ladies in Litchfield, Connecticut (est. 1819), whose high standards apparently exceeded most of the others, could claim a pupil as prominent as Harriet Beecher-Stowe (1811–1896). She attended school there between the ages of eight and thirteen and later remarked that her passion for reading and writing had been very much encouraged by her tutors.

In contrast, a few decades earlier, the author Catherine Sedgwick (1789–1867) had commented that her schooling in private academies in New York, Albany, and Boston, which "emphasized nonacademic subjects such as dancing and etiquette," had been rather dull for an intellectually alert and curious girl. The success of Sedgwick's novels (for example *A New England Tale* of 1822, *Redwood* of 1824, and *Hope Leslie* of 1827) represented an important step in the recognition of women novelists. "Of the two-hundred-odd works of fiction produced by Americans between 1779 and 1829 better than a third were written for or by women. Among the most popular of these fictions were two books written by women, Susanna Towson's *Charlotte Temple* (1794) and Hannah Foster's *The Coquette* (1797)." Novels for women were distinctly different from those for men: They had to have a moralizing message so as not to be found objectionable. Fears of the potentially damaging consequences of women reading, such as the neglect of their duties to husband and children, governed their access to reading material.

As editor of *Godey's Lady's Book* from 1837 to 1877, Sarah Josepha Hale (1788–1879) exerted a great influence on women's reading activity and their taste in literature. Hale's clever marketing strategy was to solicit the male members of households as subscribers, thereby not offending their authority. *Godey's*, a conservative periodical that never departed from the context of the domestic sphere—it favored improved education for women, but only as long as their intellectual pursuits were compatible with their household duties—enjoyed the highest circulation of any periodical (150,000 at its height) until social change and progress passed it by in the 1850s: Women had obviously had enough "embroidery instructions" by then. Women's attention shifted to publications such as *Harper's New Monthly Magazine*, which had a more liberal approach. The first edition in June of 1850 had a run of 7,500 copies and some six months later the figure had already grown to 50,000. Another significant influence was the writer Margaret Fuller (1810–1850), the first full-time book reviewer and editor of the *New York Tribune*, which send her abroad in 1846 as the United States' first woman foreign correspondent. Her most significant book, *Women in the Nineteenth Century* of 1845, was a groundbreaking plea for women's rights, in particular their right to education.

One of the most widely-read books of the time was *Uncle Tom's Cabin*. Published in March of 1852, Harriet Beecher Stowe's story sold 10,000 copies within its first week, and 300,000 copies by the year's end, more than any previous secular book, and made its author America's best paid writer. Since no international copyright law was in place yet, "an estimated one million copies of numerous pirate editions were sold in England" in addition. Beecher-Stowe's most prominent reader was Queen Victoria, and it is said that the queen wept when reading the novel. Second in popularity to *Uncle Tom's Cabin* was most likely Susan Warner's (1819–1885) *The Wide, Wide World* of 1851, a typical example of the kind of religious fiction that was extremely popular at the time. By 1852 it was in its fourteenth edition and had been translated into French, Italian, Russian, Swedish, and Spanish. Other notable women authors of the time were Mary Abigail Dodge, Luisa May Alcott, Elisa Leslie, and Elizabeth Stuart Phelps. Phelps had initially wanted to paint, but found writing easier to fit into her life as wife and mother.

"Novels for women were distinctly different from those for men: They had to have a moralizing message so as not to be found objectionable."

The wide circulation of books benefited from increased literacy; a U. S. census records the literacy rate in 1850 as being about ninety percent, although this was not broken down by gender and does not indicate exactly how literacy was measured or defined. Improvements in printing technology also made printed matter more affordable. In 1847 the American inventor Richard Hoe (1812–1886) developed a high-speed rotary press in which, unlike the old flat-bed presses, the printing surface was wrapped around a revolving cylinder, an invention that paved the way for the technologically sophisticated printing presses to come.

Technological and socio-economic changes conspired to make it increasingly difficult to control women's reading and restrict their access to books. Well to-do middle class families began staffing their households with servants, affording the mistresses more time to read as well as the opportunity to send their daughters to school, now that they were no longer needed to help in the household. Gatherings for the exchange of opinions on cultural events and literature—as seen for example in Hans Heinrich Bebie's painting *Ladies in Conversation* (page 122)—became a commonplace on the social calendar in upper middle-class households. Bebie depicts a group of Baltimore society women enjoying the company of visiting opera singer Jenny Lind. The rather conservative depiction reveals to what degree such drawing-room gatherings—and the books that were an integral part of them—had by now become socially acceptable. Informal reading groups had begun to appear in the last decades of the eighteenth century: Apart from the exchange of useful knowledge and the promotion of moral duty, these early reading societies also had the very practical function of helping women avoid the high cost of books by lending them to each other.

Just such an exchange of literary interests can be seen in the eminent British artist Sir Edward Burne-Jones' *Green Summer* (fig. 2). In the pictorial language of the Pre-Raphaelites, the artist depicts a group of women in the English countryside who have come together to read and reflect. Among its sitters might well be the beautiful Macdonald sisters, who, if nothing else, proved that being well educated and bookish in no way diminished their chances for marriage and social advancement. Indeed, this had been one of the standard arguments against a more intellectually stimulating education for women. Georgiana married Edward Burne-Jones and Agnes married his colleague Sir Edward Poynter, at one time head of the Royal Academy, the National Gallery, and the Tate simultaneously. Louisa' son Stanley Baldwin became British prime minister, and Alice was the mother of Rudyard Kipling, the first Englishman to receive the Nobel Prize for literature.

The Macdonald sisters were born into a lower middle-class family with no opportunity for formal education and few prospects of upward social mobility within the rigid social structures of early Victorian England. In this context, their prospects for the future seemed quite limited. But their father, a Methodist minister, took great pains to educate his daughters and encouraged extensive and intensive reading from his thousand-book-strong library. The girls were thus equipped with the knowledge necessary to intelligently tackle the obstacles of life and certainly did not owe their social ascent to their beauty and refined manners alone.

Julius LeBlanc Stewart's *Sarah Bernhardt and Christina Nilsson* (page 146) depicts a cultural exchange on a different level. Two of the great stars of their time, the divine actress Sarah Bernhardt and the soprano Christina Nilsson, are engaged in a discussion of literature related to their professions. The prerequisites for Sarah Bernhardt's (1844–1923) exceptional career were provided by her ambitious mother, who wanted to establish her daughter in the higher echelons of society. After two years at the renowned Institute Fressard, the Paris boarding school where Sarah learned reading, writing, and some embroidery, as well as the first steps in fine manners, she then continued against her will for another six years at the famous convent school Grandchamps, where daughters of august Parisian families were educated. It was there that Sarah received her final polish and developed a love of acting while successfully performing the role of an angel in a convent play. Christina Nilsson (1843–1921), equally successful and from an equally humble background, initially had only a very basic education but found a patron at the age of fourteen, enabling her to study in Paris.

Just as actresses and great singers captured the world's stages and concert halls in the second half of the nineteenth century, women writers too took to the literary stage as professionals. They no longer published under a male or pen name, but their own. With readers in tow, they wrote with self-confidence on various subjects in all literary genres, their works aimed at all of society even if still

2 Sir Edward Burne-Jones (1833–1898)
Green Summer, 1868
Private Collection

The circle of women is obviously listening to a moving story read to them by the figure on the left; their expressions are contemplative, even melancholic. A leading figure of the Pre-Raphaelites, Burne-Jones also used this scene in a smaller version in 1864.

predominantly intended for the woman reader. These novels by and for women retained their distinctive character: They focused almost exclusively on women's worlds and the way they lived, the clothes they wore, the food they ate, their daily gossip, and what broke their hearts; they provided their readers with things to learn from or emulate. As opposed to men's adventure stories of masculine bravery in the wilderness, of flying clippers and daring stagecoaches, women's novels gave their readers a picture of the contemporary social world (real or imagined), such as a fancy ball or dinner party. Women's books were set within the social context that surrounded and shaped their readers. But while women writers slipped in veiled lines about the injustices of women's lives, they could not yet write about this directly without facing severe criticism and arousing controversy.

Although books were now readily available and more affordable, the type of literature provided to girls and young women was still closely monitored. Books were generally purchased by men, and men were also the subscribers to libraries. Women were not considered critical enough to make the right choices, so men categorized books and kept lists of which ones to recommend or ban from women, for reading the "wrong" books could have an immoral influence or could corrupt a girl's susceptible imagination. Novels were particularly suspect on this count. Not only fathers, but mothers too were concerned. Assigned the task of moral authority in the home, mothers were particularly anxious about romantic novels, fearing their daughters would become foolish or lost in daydreaming and erotic thoughts. Hand-selecting reading material for women was therefore widely practiced as a "protective" measure. Images of women reading also depict a variety of relationships with reading material. The furtive and even provocative backward glance of James J. Tissot's protagonist in *October* (page 138) seems to presuppose this context of social control and restriction as she clearly steals away to a hiding place to read her book undisturbed. In contrast, the young woman in Winslow Homer's *The New Novel* of the same year (page 140) lies comfortably and peacefully in the grass, oblivious to her environment and immersed in her new book. The ease and naturalness of her pose exclude the possibility of anything illicit or forbidden.

By the late nineteenth century, the woman reader had, despite all obstacles, established a certain independence. But whereas reading for pleasure or recreation was common by now, the majority of women would have to wait until well into the twentieth century to pursue reading for pure intellectual or professional purposes. They would similarly have to wait for broader access to higher education. A pioneer in coeducation, Oberlin College (Ohio, est. 1833) was the first American college to admit men and women on an equal basis, and several state universities such as Michigan, California, and Wisconsin followed suit in the 1850s and 1860s; Georgia's Female College opened as early as 1839. Vassar College in Poughkeepsie, New York, exclusively for women, was founded in 1865; Smith, Wellesley (both in Massachusetts) and many more followed. While this was certainly an impressive advance, few could take advantage of it, as enrollment figures tell. In 1838 only a single woman graduated from Oberlin; in 1870, 35 did so. When Wellesley College opened in 1875, 314 women applied but only 30 were found qualified for the collegiate curriculum, not surprising at a time when few places allowed girls to attend the high schools where young men were prepared for college. Wellesley awarded its first degrees in 1879 to 18 women students. By 1900, the enrollment was 716. At Vassar the figures were 315 students in 1865 and 799 by 1900.

In comparison, in England, at Oxford's first women's college, Lady Margaret Hall (see page 52) 9 students enrolled in the first year (1879), of whom 2 studied English, 1 ancient history, and another 1 philosophy; for the remaining 5 there is no record in the register. By 1900 this number increased to a mere 17. Moreover, women students could not attend unchaperoned and they could not earn degrees; degrees for women equal to those of men were first awarded in 1920. At Cambridge, the first degree at a woman's college was awarded only in 1948. Of the approximately 1700 Ph.D.s awarded by American universities between 1861 and 1900 about 100 were awarded to women.

Paintings of women reading are numerous from the second half of the nineteenth century, reflecting increased literacy and women's connection with books. Artists depicted their models engaged in a refined sort of leisure. Wholesome activities such as reading are carried out in pleasant surroundings, elegant interiors, or gardens filled with sunlight and greenery; the woman reader is frequently placed among flowers and fields as in Claude Monet's *Springtime* (page 132), or Berthe Morisot's *Reading* (page 134). The increasing industrialization of their societies and, accompanying it, a certain alienation of the individual, are made visible by Édouard Manet in *The Railway* (page 136), in which his protagonist reads at the side of the railway tracks of the Gare Saint-Lazare. In contrast, William Merritt Chase's *In the Studio* (page 144) is set in the artist's fashionable atelier. In addition to demonstrating how splendid an artist's studio could look in the Gilded Age, Chase here depicts an unchaperoned woman visitor, who, in an even more independent gesture, seems to form her own opinion about art by leafing through a large volume of elaborate illustrations, most likely one of the artist's sketchbooks. The Australian artist James Fox paints his reader (page 168) swaying in a hammock in a moment of ultimate leisure and relaxation.

Women artists such as Berthe Morisot, Mary Cassatt, and Cecelia Beaux, still a minority and aware of their ambivalent situation in a male-dominated trade, intelligently walked a fine line between their own achievement and the resentment the public still harbored against women professionals. They very ladylike Cassatt, who had to overcome her father's objections to her career choice in the first place, concentrated on paintings that radiated the joy and delight of motherhood, as in *Family Group Reading* (page 164). Although more of a rebel by nature, in her work Cecelia Beaux also remained within the boundaries of social acceptability. In *New England Woman* (page 160) she pays tribute to the values of earlier days and evokes the atmosphere of wholesome family life. In contrast to Cassatt's family, the grandmother and aunt who raised Beaux encouraged her in her pursuits as an artist. In 1895 Beaux became the first full-time woman faculty member at the Pennsylvania Academy of the Fine Arts, the oldest art school in the United States, founded by Charles Willson Peale in 1791; there she taught academic drawing, painting, and portraiture for the next twenty years.

Although the advancement of women's independence did not progress at the same speed in the later decades of the nineteenth century as it had before and during the Civil War years, the United States was distinctly more progressive than Europe, leading a puzzled Frenchman by the name of Paul Bourget, who toured the United States in the 1890s, to ask "How does it come to pass that the men of this country—so energetic, so strong-willed, so dominating —have permitted their wives to shake off masculine authority more completely than in any other part of the world." Indeed, in certain parts of Europe, women's advancement was at best stagnating if not retreating. Wilhelm Leibl's *Three Women in Church* (page 142) takes the viewer deep into Germany's rural society and reflects the enduring importance of religious literature to rural women into the late nineteenth century. While Leibl's depiction is not a general document of women's reading activity—which certainly varied greatly between town and countryside—it is a sensitive reflection of the importance religious literature could hold for rural women. As for any believer, reading the Bible was a source of comfort, hope, and faith. But Leibl's painting also implicitly communicates the sense of duty and obedience that was expected from the German wife. Women's proper stations in life were, as the German Kaiser Wilhelm II (1859–1941) apparently pointedly stated, the "three K's": Kinder, Küche, Kirche (children, kitchen, church), an attitude that met with scarcely any opposition. Germany had practically no women's movement and no defenders of the fair sex, and its leading male philosophers —Goethe, Schopenhauer, or Nietzsche—were certainly of no help. None of these great thinkers voiced the need for a more extensive literary education for women. Although Germany had introduced compulsory primary education already during the eighteenth century—one of the first countries in the world to do so—training at the eight-year *volksschule* was rigid: Next to reading, writing, and arithmetic the emphasis was on duty, discipline, and obedience. Unless it contributed to a woman's domestic responsibilities and helped to shape an obedient character,

3 Alexander Hugo Bakker Korff (1824–1882)
Bible Reading, 1879
Gemeentemuseum, Den Haag

The painting takes the viewer into the home of a rural Dutch family; books, magazines, and newspapers are strewn around the room. The artist, however, captures the women reading the Bible together. In his smaller tableaux, which Bakker Korff started to paint around 1853 due to his failing eyesight, he frequently took as his subject women engaged in conversation, domestic duties, or communal reading.

reading was deemed a frivolity and considered a thief of time.

In contrast, and, surprisingly already five decades earlier, Philippe van Bree's *L'Atelier de Femmes Peintres* (page 116) depicts an entirely different and much more liberal world. Although women's liberties in France also experienced a setback after the revolution and its powerful feminist groups lost some of their radical edge, there were nevertheless many "Bohemians" who too challenged convention. Non-conforming women formed their own circles in drawing and painting studios and reading groups, as van Bree's work so charmingly depicts. Virtually every detail points to women's intelligence. The central model, surrounded by six artists, poses as Hercules, yet the club (Hercules' central symbol) is held up by ropes, a celebration of female intelligence as opposed to masculine muscle. Another figure reads an article on "Les St. Simoniens" in the magazine *La Femme Libre*, a reference to women's independence: the St. Simoniens were a French group advocating equality for women. Van Bree's painting of women reading, drawing, and even smoking was very unusual for the time and represents a striking exception to the general attitude, which was considerably less progressive.

Berthe Morisot, for example, found her personal freedom drastically curtailed when her sister Edma got married in 1869. Until then the two sister not only attended art classes together, but also went together to art exhibitions and museums. Social convention, however, did not allow a girl from the French upper classes to do such things alone; public life was all about manners and appearances. The curricula in schools for upper-class girls was designed accordingly. Next to basic knowledge, their training consisted of learning to display refinement and culture: a certain command of playing the piano, singing, and polite

4 John White Alexander (1856–1915)
A Quiet Hour, ca. 1901
Courtesy of the Pennsylvania Academy of the Fine Arts, Philadelphia.

The sitter, Ann Raynor Ward, posed several times for the artist; her fragile health echoes in the painting. Alexander's solid reputation on both sides of the Atlantic led to the prestigious commission for the series *Evolution of the Book* for the Library of Congress, for which he painted the murals *Manuscript Book*, *Printing Press*, *Picture Writing*, and *Hieroglyphics* in the Jefferson Building.

conversational skills. Like almost anywhere in the Western world, education prepared women to be worthy companions to their husbands, charming hostesses, good household managers, and virtuous examples for their children. A more systematic training in academic subjects was not only of secondary importance but was even deemed by some to be unsuitable. Pressure on Berthe Morisot to get married also mounted, but only some eight years later would she marry Eugene Manet, the brother of Édouard Manet. In the later decades of the nineteenth century, when reading had become an integral and accepted part of women's daily lives, images of women reading are determined more by the artist' aesthetic expression and pictorial vocabulary than by the symbolic and social meanings attached to the book.

Henri Fantin-Latour's *Two Sisters* (page 126) depicts women's domestic life in more conservative bourgeois households. One sister busies herself with fancy needlework while the other sister reads. Reading to family members was common practice on Sunday afternoons or long winter evenings: One woman would read aloud while the others quietly went about their domestic chores such as sewing and embroidering. Reading to one other, whether privately or publicly is as old as human civilization and the written word itself and its tradition stretches from ancient Greece, where educated slaves read to their mistresses, through the monasteries of the Middle Ages and the Salons of the Enlightenment to present-day book club meetings.

Renoir's two reading sisters, for example, are entirely different in spirit than those of Fantin-Latour. Renoir, a traditionalist at heart, loved to paint pretty girls, and accordingly *Les Deux Soeurs* (page 150), in which the sitters are professional models, depicts young, docile and innocent bourgeois girls sharing an intimate and relaxed, almost playful moment of reading together. Fantin-Latour's sisters are more distant, even reflective, and formal in their manner and appearance. In each case, these qualities infuse the paintings with very different feelings and give them their meaning; the books are not attributes of a refined sitter, nor are they meant to characterize her qualities. In both works, reading is now the vehicle for the two artists' very distinct pictorial expressions.

Just how diverse indeed the aesthetic expressions of contemporary Montmartre painters could be is also particularly visible in Toulouse-Lautrec's work from the same year (page 152). Literally turning his back on the conventions of the bourgeoisie, Toulouse-Lautrec paints his reader, a neighborhood girl, in an unprecedented, modern style, which in its nobility is reminiscent of classical antiquity. The Nabis also introduced mythological and mystical elements into such images, rendering the act of reading by women as something more evocative, subjective, and linked to the imagination. Sérusier's painting of a girl studying (page 154) and Denis' of reading muses (page 156) are imbued with their makers' mystical philosophy. Sérusier's reading girl recalls a Breton culture deeply steeped in Celtic folklore and although in contemporary dress, Denis's muses evoke medieval legends.

The American artist Tarbell portrays the ideal of the wholesome American girl who was expected to be unassuming *and* studious, while his contemporary Paxton depicts a housemaid eager to educate herself even if it meant prying into her employer's books (pages 168, 170). Working-class girls could not yet afford to buy books. Many of these women indeed used part of their meager incomes for library memberships. Only smaller libraries admitted

5 Rupert Charles Wulsten Bunny (1864–1947)
Woman Reading, ca. 1907
Private Collection

Bunny's reader is his beautiful French wife and favorite model, Jeanne Heloise (née Morel) whom he married in 1902. At the time they met she was an art student, exhibiting at the Old Salon, but later gave up her art in favor of her husband. The book might be a French classic, for Mrs. Bunny did not speak (or read) English.

women; the larger ones denied them membership until the late nineteenth or early twentieth centuries, and even then women were whisked off into separate reading rooms.

From the mid nineteenth century on, paintings of women reading—although portraying only a narrow segment of society, mainly the upper-class—demonstrate that although society as a whole was still anxious about the adverse effects of reading on women's minds and social responsibilities, the woman reader is no longer marginalized. Control of women's access to reading material could no longer be exercised as thoroughly as in previous decades; more and more women determined for themselves what they would read. They had, so to speak, irrevocably connected with books.

While the images in this chapter do not simply reflect social and historical changes, they are nonetheless a part of them. The significance of leisure as an agent of social change can be seen clearly reflected in the paintings of the nineteenth century. In the twentieth century the subject matter of women reading becomes less and less a social statement and—like all figurative subject matter—increasingly a vehicle for aesthetic experimentation. These experiments will endow the subject matter of women reading with new meaning and associations and integrate it into the innovations of twentieth-century art.

5 Sir John Lavery (1856–1941)
Miss Auras, The Red Book, ca. 1902
Philip Mould Ltd., London

When Lavery met the sitter, the sixteen-year-old Mary Auras in 1901, he was so taken by her beauty that he immediately embarked on a series of half-length portraits of which the present one is considered the most important. Her gesture as she angles the slim volume is full of alacrity; the book' scarlet cover forms a piquant contrast to Mary's white dress. The Irish-born Lavery was associated with the Glasgow School (he initially studied there) and was elected to the Royal Academy in London in 1921 and knighted in the same year. *The Red Book* resonates *Symphony in White no.2* (Tate Britain) by his friend Whistler, although here its melancholy is replaced by Mary's vitality and poise.

The First African-American Woman Poet

Phillis Wheatley Writing
Cover page of her book
Poems of 1773
Engraving by Scipio
Moorhead (fl. 1770s)

The full title of Phillis' book is *Poems on Various Subjects, Religious and Moral*; an inscription below her image states: "published according to Act of Parliament, Sept. 1, 1773 by Arch. Bell, Bookseller no. 8 near the Saracens Head, Aldgate." Published in London, the book caused a small sensation on both sides of the Atlantic. Her deeply moving verse—many of her poems were on life's hardships and the deaths of family members, in particular infants—was prefaced by the novelty of her image on the book: The printed image of a female slave, or indeed of any individual American woman, was exceedingly rare. Because people doubted her authorship—how could a slave girl write so eloquently?—a testimony of authenticity underwritten by sixteen Boston dignitaries was printed in the book.

Phillis (ca. 1753–1784) was purchased by the Wheatley family, a cultured household, who soon discovered the girl's abilities and gave her time to study, something unthinkable for a slave girl. Her first poem "On Messr. Hussey and Coffin," was the story of two fisherman caught up in a deadly storm at sea and saved by their steady faith in God. An elegy on the death of the popular minister Rev. George Whitefield on September 1770, printed in a number of colonial newspapers, brought her public recognition. Phillis' literary works were an expression of her Puritan upbringing, reflecting the values and culture of New England at the time. She did, however, voice some sentiments about the issue of slavery. In the 1830s, abolitionists reprinted her poetry; her life was to become an inspiration to future generations of African-Americans.

The artist, Scipio Moorehead, was the slave of the pastor John Moorehead and learned his skills as a draughtsman from his owner's wife, the art teacher Sarah Moorehead. The drawing, in which Phillis' dress clearly identifies her as a slave, apparently resembled the author very closely.

PHILLIS WHEATLEY, NEGRO SERVANT to Mr. JOHN WHEATLEY, of BOSTON.

The Emblem Book

Charles Willson Peale
(1741–1827)
Mrs. Samuel Mifflin
and Her Granddaughter
Rebecca Mifflin Francis,
1777–80
The Metropolitan Museum
of Art New York

Detail
It was customary to educate girls at home and emblem books were a favored instrument.

The painting unmistakably represents the custom of the day: Girls were taught and trained at home. The title of the book, *Emblems, for the Entertainment and Improvement of Youth* (1735), summarizes the customary subject matter of their instruction at the time. Obviously a loving grandmother, Mrs. Mifflin rests her arm protectively on the shoulder of the child and her face radiates warmth and filial love. The book's pedagogical function is emphasized by the girl's pointing finger, which draws attention to the emblem "On Love & Duty." A kind of "picture book," emblem books combined illustrations (mostly woodcuts) with practical explanations and often included a biblical citation. Emblem books first appeared in Europe during the sixteenth century and were both secular and religious in nature.

Born in Queen Anne's County, Maryland Charles Willson Peale was an exponent of America's first portrait movement. His style of portraying his sitters with naturalistic features and expressions evoking philosophical contemplation greatly appealed to his clients from the rural gentry. In the present portrait, Mrs. Mifflin is depicted in her own clothes in contrast to the usual practice of painting the sitter with imaginary clothing; her quilted blue satin underskirt is now in the Philadelphia Museum of Art.

Shaping Taste

Ralph Earl (1751–1801)
Esther Boardman, 1789
The Metropolitan Museum of Art New York

Seated in a landscape, the stylishly dressed Esther Boardman holds a slim book, most likely of poetry, a reference to her virtues and sensibilities and the cultured household of the Boardman family. Her fancy headdress is made of black and white feathers and, as was customary among stylish women of the late eighteenth century, Esther accentuated the fashionable paleness of her face with eyebrows made from the skin of a mouse.

While Esther is depicted as a delicate, almost fragile young lady, her brother's portraits by Earl of the same year depict men in command of their trades: The elder brother Daniel figures as the gentleman landowner he was, and Elijah, as the successful dry-goods merchant and man of cultivation in front of his counting desk, whose top and shelves are filled with books. An open door shows the viewer the inside of his shop with bolts of silk and other fine textiles. Among the books on the shelves are three volumes of Dr. John Moore's *Travel*, two volumes of Shakespeare's plays, John Milton's *Paradise Lost*, Samuel Johnson's dictionary, and the *London Magazine* from 1786. It can be assumed that Esther Boardman would have had access to most of these books.

Like most American painters who ventured to London, the self-taught Ralph Earl too refined his style there under Reynolds, Copley, and West. His paintings became smoother, as opposed to his early, actually very attractive, "stiffness." By the time he returned to New York in 1785 Earl had lost all his money as a result of "bad spending habits" and was confined to a debtor's prison for over a year. It was in fact Eliza Hamilton, wife of the founding father Alexander Hamilton, who helped him out by sitting for a portrait (*Elisabeth Schuyler Hamilton*, 1787, now at the Museum of the City of New York) and urging her friends to do the same. Earl painted around twenty portraits of prominent people while in prison.

Detail
The small book, most likely of poetic inspiration, communicates the sitter's virtues and sensibilities.

Intellectual Prowess

John Opie (1761–1807)
Mary Wollstonecraft
(Mrs. William Godwin),
ca. 1790–97
Tate London

Mary Wollstonecraft (1759–1797) argued tirelessly and without fear of ridicule for the rights of women. Her most important work, *A Vindication of the Rights of Women*, was a bold call for a radically new attitude to women's abilities and rights. Like an echo of Christine de Pizan's sentiments in *Citè des Dames*, Wollstonecraft urged her audience to acknowledge that women were not inferior but possessed just as much natural intelligence as men and lacked only the chance for a proper education. A radical thinker, Wollstonecraft campaigned not only for the rights of women, but was concerned with the state of mankind in general. She advocated for democratic social structures, opposed hereditary rights, criticized the "immoral" treatment of the poor, condemned slavery, and regarded the monarchy and the church as oppressive.

The portrait shows Wollstonecraft as if interrupted in her work. Despite her status as an intellectual icon this was quite remarkable for a time when the representation of intellectual prowess was exclusively reserved for portraits of men. John Opie, a good friend of Mary Wollstonecraft, was a largely self-trained artist from Cornwall known for the contrast of light and dark that he used to great effect. None of the famous and fashionable portraitists of the time painted Mary Wollstonecraft, which is not surprising given the fact that rather than frequenting aristocratic soirees, she met with friends in pubs or coffeehouses, the watering holes of the avant-garde and radical thinkers. She was everything other than a typical Salon beauty.

Les Femmes Libres

Philippe van Bree
(1786–1871)
The Studio of Women Painters, ca. 1831
Musee des Beaux Arts de Belgium, Brussels

Detail
The young woman reads an article on the St. Simoniens, a feminist group advocating for women's equality.

In van Bree's work a group of women challenges traditional gender roles. The elegantly attired protagonists not only "band together" in solidarity, they also smoke, draw, paint, read the intellectual journal *La Femme Libre,* and one even assumes the guise of Hercules. The female model posing as Hercules represents Omphale, Queen of Lydia, who bought Hercules as a slave and, upon discovering his true identity, married and traded clothes with him; she donned the lion skin and club, classic symbols of masculinity and power, but did not usurp his role. Here, female intelligence and sensuality do not contradict each other: As her attire and bare breast attest, she remains very much a sensuous woman. Van Bree is also careful to show that the central symbol of Hercules, the club, is held up by ropes, a reference to female intelligence as opposed to masculine muscle. The entire painting is a celebration of women's intelligence.

On the wall behind, to the right, is a self-portrait by Vigée-Le Brun and to the left most likely one by Lavinia Fontana or Artemisia Gentileschi. The model seated below is reading an article about the St. Simoniens, a French group advocating equality for women.

This unusual painting has been published several times with differing interpretations. Van Bree, who studied first with his brother and then at the Academy of Anvers, went to Paris in 1811 and quickly made a name for himself at the Paris Salons. He became famous for his interiors of artists' studios, allowing him to paint the sumptuous objects and beautiful models found there.

Patroness of Education

Sir William Charles Ross
(1794–1860)
Angela Georgina, Baroness
Burdett-Coutts, ca. 1847
National Portrait Gallery,
London

The son of Queen Victoria, Edward VII, called Angela Burdett-Coutts (1814–1906) the most remarkable woman in the country after his mother. The fabulously rich Burdett-Coutts was determined to use part of her wealth to help the disadvantaged. She spent between three to four million pounds on charities, of which a large portion was dedicated to improving the pitiful conditions of destitute children and orphans as well as for vocational training for unskilled and "fallen" women. During the baroness's lifetime, she was one of the very few advocates of broad public education. At the time, middle-class girls received all or most of their education at home. Education did not become a real priority in English social legislation until 1870, the year of the first Education Act.

Burdett-Coutts' advisor in her social crusade was none other than Charles Dickens. The versatile Dickens was also editor of the journal *Household Words* in which, in addition to treating political subjects, he demanded reforms in health and education.

William Charles Ross was appointed miniature painter to Queen Victoria in 1837 and this position brought him many portrait commission from royal circles. The pensive pose in which the artist portrays Angela Burdett-Coutts, and the amount of paperwork on the desk are a clear reference to her social concerns and activities.

Russia's Schools for Girls

Christina Robertson
(1796–1854)
Portrait of Grand Duchess
Maria Alexandrovna,
ca. 1849
State Hermitage Museum
St. Petersburg

The German-born Grand Duchess Maria Alexandrovna (1824–1880), wife of Emperor Alexander II, devoted her entire life to the education of women and other charitable concerns. She set up public schools for girls from all social backgrounds and made it mandatory for diocesan schools to open their doors to girls as well. The duchess fostered several democratic reforms and the curricula in the schools she founded were remarkably diverse.

Until the late seventeenth century Russian women of royal lineage led a life of seclusion, uneducated and absolutely barred from public life; even when attending church, they had to be veiled and sit behind a screen. A library list of the possessions of Peter the First's unmarried sister, the Tsarevna Natalia Alexeevna (1673–1716), who was much better educated than probably any other royal women of her time, lists 110 books predominantly of religious subject matter. The peasant women (the peasant population in Russia comprised ninety-five percent of the population), most of them serfs, remained at an educational level probably comparable to the early Middle Ages in Europe.

A change in women's social status first took place under the enlightened Catharine II (1720–1796). Russia's first girls' school, the Smolny Institute for Gentlewomen, was founded in 1764. The recorded literacy rate of forty-one percent of noblewomen in 1750–55, and ninety-two percent between 1805–1819 must be viewed in light of the fact that these figures were based on the woman's ability to sign her name in official records (while women had virtually no rights, they could own property). Most women at the time were completely uneducated.

Christina Robertson, the first female member of the Royal Scottish Academy, worked repeatedly in Russia between 1839 and the late 1840s. Her main patrons were members of the imperial household. This portrait was commissioned by Tsar Nicholas I, Duchess Alexandrovna's father-in-law.

Christina Robertson pinx

Drawing-Room Gatherings

Hans Heinrich Bebie (1800–1888)
Ladies in Conversation, 1850–55
Private Collection
Courtesy Hirschl & Adler Galleries, New York

In stark contrast to van Bree's group of women challenging social convention (page 116), Bebie's painting offers the comforting reassurance of a traditional women's social gathering; there is nothing radical going on here. Regardless of their social and geographical background, women did form their own circles, however their gatherings were social events rather than intellectual study groups. The latter would follow towards the end of the century.

The elegantly dressed and coiffed ladies concentrate their attention on the seated woman with the open book. She seems to have paused in her reading aloud, perhaps to discuss or explain some aspect of the text. It has been suggested that the woman reading may well be the famous nineteenth-century opera singer Jenny Lind (1820–1887), who may have visited Baltimore or a nearby city during her sensational and legendary ninety-stop tour in America from 1850 to 1852. Two of the models seem to want to give her a letter or a little note, maybe in appreciation of her performance. Lind, also called the "Swedish Nightingale," never forgot her humble origins and donated large parts of her fortune to poor musicians, hospitals, and orphanages. San Francisco's first opera house was named after her.

Born in Switzerland, Bebie arrived on American shores in 1842, settling first in Virginia and then in Baltimore, Maryland, where he remained until his death. He is best known today for pictures of women conversing in interiors. Bebie enjoyed representing the drama of human interaction in a variety of social circumstances and there has been speculation among scholars that some of his interiors depict illicit soirees in brothels, where anonymous men and women of the demimonde interacted.

Essays in Idleness

Gakutei Harunobu,
(fl. ca. 1813–ca. 1868)
Two Geisha reading from a book, Japan, Edo period, Nineteenth century
Freer Gallery of Art, Smithsonian Institution, Washington, DC

The two lavishly dressed courtesans read from the *Tsurezuregusa* (*Essays in Idleness*), a classical work by the Japanese Buddhist monk Yoshida Kenko (1283–1350). The image is set in their private rooms next to a circular window and cherry blossoms fall from trees in full bloom.

In Japanese culture, the geisha employed her skills as a musician, dramatist, artist, and conversationalist to entertain men in special venues where they gathered to socialize and conduct business. Among the highest-ranking professional entertainers in the licensed pleasure district of Edo, geishas were famous not only for their beauty but also for their cultivation of literary pursuits and their knowledge of the arts such as calligraphy. The training of a traditional geisha was very rigorous and it took many years until she attained the perfection expected from her. A geisha was probably as well read as any woman of the highest nobility. A more modern Japanese ideal of womanhood emerged at the end of the nineteenth and beginning of the twentieth centuries, although primary education for girls and boys had been decreed by law in 1872. By 1876, for example, Tokyo's Women's Normal School was training women as elementary school teachers. The first medical school for women was founded in 1900, and the first women's college in 1901.

Gakutei was a native of Edo (present-day Tokyo), who became a poet, painter, and designer of prints, especially privately commissioned *surimono*. His treatment of the figures and their costumes betray his interest in Hokusai's style.

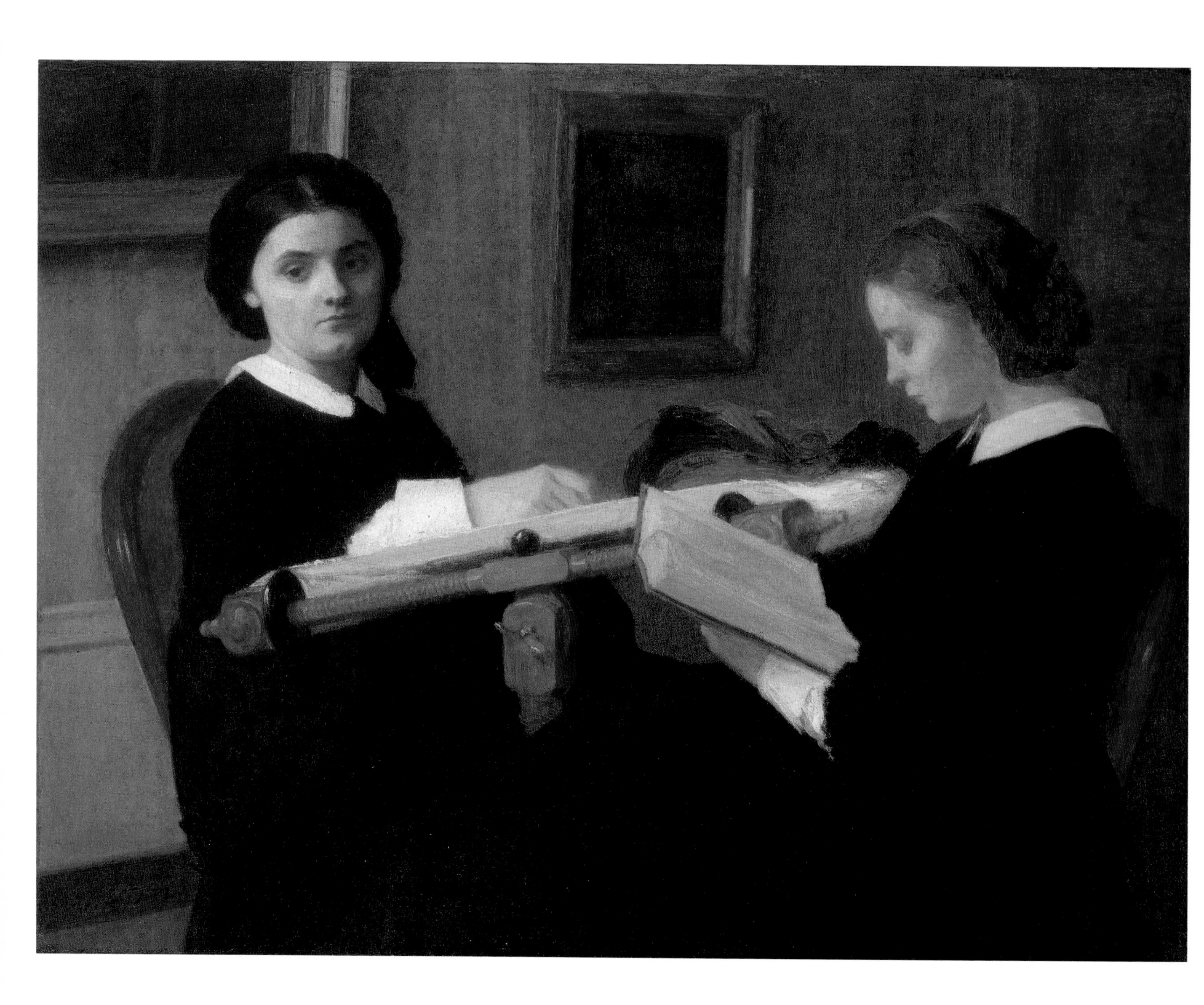

Sunday Afternoon

Henri Fantin-Latour
(1836–1904)
The Two Sisters, 1859
The Saint Louis Art
Museum, St. Louis

Fantin-Latour's favorite models were the female members of his family; he painted this portrait of his two sisters in the intimate setting of their home when he was only twenty-two. Natalie, on the left, is engaged in the traditional activity of needlework while Marie is absorbed in reading a book. This scene of exemplary conduct most likely takes place on a Sunday afternoon when families traditionally shared leisurly hours together: Often one family member would read aloud while the others would quietly busy themselves with "the domestic arts" such as needlepoint as they listened. Such communal and recreational reading was practiced not only in affluent households but throughout society. The nature of the book might vary according to social class and from rural to urban areas, but it was always some kind of morally uplifting literature that might have been selected by the father or mother of the household.

The strong colors of the wool on the embroidery frame form a striking contrast to the severity of the two sisters' black-and-white dresses. Fantin-Latour used the same tranquil setting in his painting *Women Reading* of 1861 (Musée d'Orsay, Paris), for which, given her resemblance to the sitter in the present painting, his sister Marie must also have been the model. Another depiction of the meditative quality and tranquility of reading, a frequent subject in Fantin-Latour's early oeuvre, is the portrait of his wife, the painter Victoria Dubourg of 1873, in which she is reading from a large volume. The two met at the Louvre in the mid 1860s. Unfortunately the book she is reading could not be identified in any of the paintings.

Whereas today it is his exquisite still lifes—in which flowers and fruits were treated almost like portraits—that primarily capture the art connoisseur's attention, during his life Henri Fantin-Latour was actually a greatly sought-after portraitist, especially in Britain.

The Music Room

James McNeill Whistler
(1834–1903)
Harmony in Green and Rose: the Music Room, 1860–1861
Freer Gallery of Art, Smithsonian Institution, Washington, DC

Harmony in Green and Rose is one of Whistler's first paintings of modern life, set in the music room of the London house of his half-sister Deborah Delano Haden, the wife of a prominent surgeon. The seated girl reading a large book is the artist's niece Annie Haden. Annie's figure is isolated, even physically removed from the other figures, emphasizing the solitary nature of her activity. The image of her mother in riding dress is reflected in the mirror: Isabella Boott, daughter of the founder of the town of Lowell, Massachusetts, had married Haden's younger brother. The picture is thus emblematic of Whistler's family ties in both America and Britain and it reflects the lifestyle of the well-to-do and their intention of educating their daughters well; reading matter is readily available here.

Harmony in Green and Rose is an impressive display of Whistler's maturing style and an example of the visual analogies between Whistler and Velasquez; the flatness of the image space also reflects Whistler's fascination with Japanese art. Although Whistler, one of the greatest artists of his time, cultivated a reputation as an eccentric flaneur or dandy and had a turbulent romantic life, he was nevertheless a conservative man. In his own painting school he had separate studios for male and female students—and no drawing from nude models.

Famous Poetry

Sir Edward Burne-Jones (1833–1898)
Laus Veneris, 1873–75
Laing Art Gallery, Tyne & Wear Museums

The subject is derived from the well-known poem "Laus Veneris" by the famous British poet Algernon Charles Swinburne (1837–1909) in *Poems and Ballads,* first published in 1866. Originally based on the medieval legend of Tannhäuser, "Laus Veneris" evokes the Victorian fascination with the Middle Ages. Swinburne's *Poems and Ballads,* dedicated to Burne-Jones, caused a sensation and scandal at the same time because of its erotic subject matter, in particular the poems written in homage to Sappho. By 1868, the volume was already in its third edition.

Considered by many one of Burne-Jones' best works, this painting shows the legendary court of Venusberg, or the city of love; the queen's women are playing music (known as the food of love). A rose, also a symbol of love, lies on the ground near the queen. The tapestry in the background shows Cupid riding on the chariot of Venus, the goddess of love.

The leader of the second phase of the Pre-Raphaelite movement, Burne-Jones took the rather pedantic medievalism of the early Pre-Raphaelites and turned it into an idiom altogether his own. His work exerted a very strong influence on the development of English art during the second half of the nineteenth century and continued to have an impact on the artists of the late Victorian Age, such as Lord Leighton and Sir Poynter, the brother-in-law of his wife and, at one time, head of the Royal Academy, the National Gallery, and the Tate simultaneously. Burne-Jones also worked as a book illustrator, for example of the medieval story *Le Morte d'Arthur;* the young Aubrey Beardsley followed in his footsteps. The latter's illustrations for the play *Salome* by his contemporary Oscar Wilde established Beardsley as one of the founders of Art Nouveau.

Detail
Victorian England was fascinated by the legends of the Middle Ages.

Summer Reading

Claude Monet (1840–1926)
Springtime (La Liseuse), 1872
The Walters Art Museum, Baltimore

Claude Monet portrays his wife Camille seated on the lawn in serene absorption in her book. The motif and the delicacy of her form are reminiscent of eighteenth-century representations of women reading. The location is the garden of Maison Aubry, Monet's first domicile in Argenteuil, a suburb of Paris on the Seine River where Monet and his wife stayed from 1871 onwards before eventually settling in Giverny.

Setting women (or children) among flowers and fields was a popular compositional device because of the association of women and children with nature. In his Impressionist language, Monet bathes his reader in pastel colors and sunlight, surrounded by lush foliage; in a pose of exquisite tranquility Camille, her eyes lowered, concentrates on the book. Her voluminous pink dress seems to float over the grass. Mary Cassatt adored the painting and actually owned it for a while around 1889.

Paintings of women reading are numerous in the second half of the nineteenth century and reflect the rise of the bourgeoisie, who had the financial means to support their interests in the arts and literature as well as the leisure to read. Reading was now considered beneficial to women, but only as long as the selected literature was not morally questionable.

The Educated Sisters

Berthe Morisot (1841–1895)
Reading, 1873
The Cleveland Museum of Art

On the prompting of their mother, Berthe Morisot and her two sisters received an education appropriate to their social class, which included lessons in the various arts such as piano and singing as well as instruction in drawing and watercolor techniques, given by private tutors. This kind of education, however, was not intended to lead to any professional activity but rather to equip the girls with cultural refinement. Manners and appearances ruled everyday life.

The Morisot sisters' talent was first discovered by Joseph-Benoit Guichard (a follower of both Ingres and Delacroix), who ran an art school for girls close to the Morisots' home. Guichard was particularly interested in the education of girls (from 1868 until his death in 1880 he would direct a municipal course in drawing and painting for girls in Lyons). When Berthe and Edma returned from their first lesson they were filled with enthusiasm (the eldest sister, however, decided not to pursue such training any further.) After three years of studio work under Guichard the two sisters then studied plein air painting under Corot, who in fact feared for the girls' innocence since they displayed such serious commitment (Edma would eventually give up her interest in painting in favor of marriage). The chief formative influence in Berthe Morisot's professional life was that of Édouard Manet, her brother-in-law. Supported by the Impressionist artist, she exhibited in seven of their eight exhibitions and was the first woman painter to do so. It could be speculated that Morisot's great talent was inherited: her great grandfather was no less than the famous eighteenth-century French painter Jean-Honoré Fragonard.

Berthe Morisot frequently painted women reading outdoors. The reader in Morisot's painting is her sister Edma, and the work is set in the park-like garden of her sister's estate in Maurecourt, near Auvers, northwest of Paris.

Urban Life

Édouard Manet (1832–1883)
The Railway, 1873
National Gallery of Art, Washington, DC

Detail
Both the lap dog and the book are expressions of affluence and leisure.

The painting is dominated by two figures—Victorine Meurent, one of Manet's favorite models, and the daughter of his neighbor Alphonse Hirsch—placed on the edge of the street overlooking the tracks near the Pont de l'Europe. The standing child looks out on the tracks while the seated woman looks up from her reading as if to acknowledge a passer-by, yet in a very impersonal and detached manner. With the title *Railway*, Manet does not give any direct indication of who the sitters are, for it is the modern Paris that he is painting, its urban life and the mobility brought about by the industrial revolution, but also the impersonal, fleeting moment, in short, contemporary life in a modern city. As a result this is not a painting of a "mother and child," but of two "models" placed side by side against the backdrop of the modern city.

In 1871 Manet had taken up residence at the rue Saint Petersburg very close to the eastern tracks of the Pont l'Europe, part of the Gare Saint-Lazare. A master of psychological realism and the acknowledged father of Impressionism, Manet painted scenes of modern life modeled along the lines of traditional compositions with his main formative influence being the art of Velasquez; in the present painting this is particularly visible in the composition of the child. One of Édouard Manet's greatest achievements, *The Railway* was first exhibited in 1874 at the Paris Salon, his exhibition site for years.

Stealing Away

James-Jacques-Joseph Tissot (1836–1902)
October, 1877
The Montreal Museum of Fine Arts

Though reading became a more widespread activity in the second half of the nineteenth century, books for young ladies were often still hand-selected by their parents or husbands.

In the present painting, the young woman seems to be stealing away to a hiding place. Is the book under her arm one of those "dangerous novels" she should not read, the type parents feared would endanger the virtues of their daughters? If so, such (doubtful) precaution was too late for the sitter, Kathleen Newton (1854–1882), who by the age of eighteen had already been through quite an ordeal. The daughter of Anglo-Irish parents, she was shipped out to India for an arranged marriage to a British civil servant, fell in love during the ocean crossing, bore an illegitimate child, married nonetheless, had another child, was shipped back to England and divorced, all in roughly two years.

Kathleen Newton was the companion and muse of Tissot, with whom she moved in shortly after they met in 1876. In this allegorical representation of autumn, she is wearing an exquisitely embroidered coat with fine fur trim. The artist painted Kathleen several times in this costume, as in *Mavourneen* (an Irish expression for "my darling") of the same year, now in a private collection. Tissot was a gifted observer of the nuances of social behavior and his great success was due in large part to his stylish and often mysterious compositions of young women.

Complete Absorption

Winslow Homer
(1836–1910)
The New Novel, 1877
Michele and Donald D'Amour Museum of Fine Arts, Springfield, Massachusetts

Comfortably stretched out on the grass the young woman has slipped away to devote herself fully to *The New Novel*. Homer clearly depicts her essentially private activity here as something self-evident without any hint of the forbidden or illicit; the woman's pose is relaxed and absorbed. Nothing is known of the model, who did not appear again in Homer's paintings after 1878, which gave rise to speculation that an unrequited love could be the reason. Homer never married but devoted his life to painting in his secluded house on the coast of Maine.

The New Novel marks the beginning of Winslow Homer's mature watercolor style and his use of a palette absent in earlier paintings, in particular the vibrant orange. By using cool and warm greens and particular shades of yellows and oranges, he imbues the light-filled scene with warmth and charm.

Born in Boston, Homer initially apprenticed as a commercial illustrator, which led to his successful freelance work with *Harper's Weekly* in New York. In 1867 he lived in Paris for almost the entire year and he had his first, quite successful watercolor exhibition in 1874.

Reading as Solace

Wilhelm Maria Hubertus Leibl (1844–1900)
Three Women in Church, 1878–1881/82
Hamburger Kunsthalle

Detail
The old woman is reading the Ash Wednesday prayer in von Cochem's *Golden Heaven = Key.*

The German Realist Hubertus Leibl moved to the Bavarian village of Aibling in 1878 in order to work on this painting in the nearby church of Berbling where local women modeled for him. In a letter to his mother of 26 October 1878 Leibl wrote: "I am painting a young and two old women, seated at the confessional. All of them are wearing local peasant costumes (Miesbacher Garb), which are very beautiful, especially on the young women. I cannot comprehend why no one has yet portrayed these people. What I have achieved so far was terribly laborious." In fact it would take Leibl four years to complete the painting, which is his masterpiece.

While the young woman is reading a smaller prayer book, the old farmer's wife reads a larger one, in fact a late edition of Martin von Cochem's *Goldener Himmel = Schlüssel* (Golden Heaven = Key); the open page is the Ash Wednesday prayer. Compared, for example, to Stewart's painting of Sarah Bernhardt and Christine Nilsson, the two representations are a world apart. Artists in different geographical regions connected with different societies, and in the case of Leibl, he connected with the farm community. Leibl's women do not read the Bible for lack of other literature or just because their society dictated it; they chose to read it, even with devotion, for the comfort and solace it provided, just as today.

The Independent Visitor

William Merritt Chase
(1849–1916)
In the Studio, ca. 1880–82
Brooklyn Museum

The visitor in Chase's lavishly decorated studio in the famous Tenth Street Studio Building is a woman engaged in a dialogue with the arts. Although the young lady is dressed in old-fashioned clothing reminiscent of the 1820s and 1830s, she is depicted as an entirely independent woman. She visits the studio alone, without the company of a chaperon and—as she leafs through the pages of a large folio spread out on the floor—she seems to form her own opinion of the elaborate illustrations in the volume, most likely a sketchbook by Chase. A leading artist in late nineteenth-century America, William Merritt Chase treated the subject of the studio in a number of paintings in which he addressed the idea of engagement with art.

Inspired by the exotically decorated studios of his European contemporaries, Chase had embarked on a collecting foray himself and some of these eclectic objects, accrued mostly during his visit to Europe, can be seen in the present painting. Above the young lady to the right, for example, is the painting of the so-called witch of Haarlem, *Malle Babbe*, now in the Metropolitan Museum of Art, New York. At the time it was thought to be the original by Frans Hals painted around 1633–1635 but in fact turned out to be a copy of around 1725–50. The poor wretched madwoman was confined to the workhouse in Haarlem, which also served as a mental asylum and prison and was partly financed by the Elisabeth Hospital (see page 68). Frans Hals' mentally ill son was one of the inmates. Chase admired Hals for bringing his countrymen to life through portraiture, and even owned one of his most famous paintings: *The Regentesses of the Old Men's Almhouse in Haarlem*, 1664, now in the Frans Hals Museum.

Chase's studio, a display of his cosmopolitanism and a showcase for his aesthetics, became the haunt of colleagues, patrons, and the broader public, to whom it was opened on a weekly basis, as well as a much publicized setting for musical and literary gatherings.

Cultural Exchange

Julius LeBlanc Stewart
(1855–1919)
Sarah Bernhardt and
Christina Nilsson, 1883
Private Collection

Two great voices of their time, one a singer, the other an actress, are shown in conversation; this is a truly enchanting and encouraging representation of women enjoying intellectual freedom. While the personalities of the two stars were quite different, they were bound together by their intellectual pursuits and their love of the arts. Sarah seems to be reading to Christina here; perhaps she is rehearsing her next role or perhaps the two ladies are exchanging opinions, a theory suggested by the presence of additional books on the chair to the side.

After completing her education at the famous convent school Grandchamps, Sarah Bernhardt (1844–1923) actually contemplated entering a convent, but thanks to Alexander Dumas, had her stage debut at the Comédie Francaise in 1862 with the title role in *Iphigenie*. By the 1880s she was performing on all the important stages of Europe and the United States. Her brilliant performances and her famous voice, unlike any other, earned her titles such as "the divine Sarah" (Oscar Wilde) and "the golden voice." Her dramatic performance in the role of Marguerite in *Camille* (*La Dame aux Camélias*, by Dumas) gained her immortal fame. The most famous actress of the late nineteenth and early twentieth centuries, Bernhardt took a great interest in the advancement of women and coached many young ladies in the art of acting. Equally successful, Christina Nilsson's career as a soprano took off after her debut at the Theátre Lyrique in Paris as Violetta in Verdi's *La Traviata* in 1864. Nilsson (1843–1921) sang at all the major opera houses from London, St. Petersburg, Vienna, to New York.

The son of a wealthy American immigrant and art collector, Julius LeBlanc Stewart was quickly integrated into the fashionable and intellectual circles in Paris. He studied with Gerome at the École des Beaux Arts. His personal friendship with Sarah Bernhardt made this painting possible.

A Pensive Mood

Thomas Eakins (1844–1916)
The Artist's Wife and His Setter Dog, ca. 1884–1889
The Metropolitan Museum of Art, New York

The sitter, Susan Macdowell (1851–1938), was one of her future husband's most gifted pupils at the Pennsylvania Academy of Arts, where she won a number of prizes in the academy's annual exhibition. The two met in 1876 and after they got married in 1884, Susan Macdowell concentrated her energy on her marriage and her husband's success rather than pursuing her own career. She returned to painting only after his death.

Like many of Eakins' portraits of women, that of his wife too has a touch of melancholy. Mrs. Eakins' pose and facial expression are very pensive. Whether her mood reflects the story she is reading in the book, from which she pauses briefly, or her discovery that her husband felt spiritually more at home in the company of young men remains speculative. Eakins' most famous paintings are of men of science or athletic young men bursting with energy during activities such as rowing, sailing, playing baseball, or swimming, as in the famous and slightly homoerotic painting *Swimming* at the Amon Carter Museum in Fort Worth.

One of America's indisputably great painters, as head of the Pennsylvania Academy of Fine Arts in Philadelphia, Thomas Eakins revolutionized art education by making scientific anatomy courses mandatory. He also supported women's art education, yet in a letter to the president of the academy he stated that while women's work was good enough to be continued, he did not believe that they would ever produce great painting or sculpture. Eakins' progressive teaching practices, which included drawing from live nude models and having the students pose for one another if models were not available, became a source of serious concern. Contemporaries feared for women students' loss of innocence through their exposure to male nudes. The board dismissed Eakins, a decision he never quite came to terms with.

The Two Sisters

Pierre-Auguste Renoir
(1841–1919)
The Two Sisters, 1889
Private Collection

Not only Renoir's patrons but also his fellow artists admired his paintings of young bourgeois girls of sweet docility and innocent allure, often presented in harmonious groupings. The two young women, professional models whose identity is not known, are captured in a moment of tender exchange in the concentrated activity of reading; they reappear as models in at least ten more paintings, for example in *Leçon de piano* of the same year.

Renoir, who lived in the middle of the avant-garde movement and was not adverse to its lifestyle, was not much interested in the realities of the Montmartre. He preferred to paint pretty young girls, idealizing them and their virtues, virtues of little interest to the avant-garde scene. No other artist has depicted so many women engaged in the act of reading (be it verse or music), which is all the more interesting in light of suggestions that Renoir did not think women should read much. For Renoir the book was obviously a stylistic device for the communication of intimacy. His paintings of the dance hall of the Moulin de la Galette are also more innocent (and sweet) than those of his contemporaries. On the subject of paintings he stated, "To my mind a picture should be something agreeable, cheerful—and yes!—nice to look at."

The son of a tailor from Limoges, Renoir started an apprenticeship as a decorator of factory-made porcelain at the age of thirteen and emerged as an important contributor to Impressionism with some of the finest portraits of the era.

The Formal Element

Henri Toulouse-Lautrec
(1864–1901)
Étude (Hélène Vary), 1889
Kunsthalle Bremen

The young Hélène Vary lived in the neighborhood of Henri Toulouse-Lautrec on the Montmartre. Her pure beauty and noble features did not escape the artist's attention; it made him even forget that she was not a redhead and he was determined to translate her qualities onto canvas. Lautrec was fascinated by Hélène's noble Grecian profile, which he described as "incomparable" and painted several times, as in *The Reader* of 1890.

The stretchers and canvases that fill the composition of *Étude* (an incredibly modern arrangement in itself) indicate that Hélène is posing in Lautrec's studio in the rue Caulaincourt. By playing with tone and color and offsetting the girl's lovely chestnut brown hair against the slightly darker large canvas behind her, Lautrec masterfully heightens both the purity of her profile and her elegant bearing. The simulated book with open pages placed in the sitter's lap demonstrates how the presence of a book gives the portrait an additional dimension: In the present painting it acts to further emphasize the sitter's nobility.

The aristocratic Toulouse-Lautrec, whose life was profoundly affected by his inborn physical abnormalities and an accident in 1878 in which he broke his left femur, was a central figure of the society of the demimonde, the world of the dance halls, circuses, and brothels. His unique work is an important document and interpretation of the culture of the marginalized Parisian proletariat at the fin de siècle, and his candid, psychologically penetrating studies, comparable to episodes from Zola's novels, appealed to artists and collectors who appreciated an art based upon the realities of modern life.

The Riddles of Grammar

Paul Sérusier (1865–1927)
French
Grammar (Study), 1892
Musée d'Orsay, Paris

A young Breton girl bent over the open pages of an oversized volume seems to be tackling the riddles of grammar. Two more large books are stacked on the left corner of the table. The semicircular painting may have been part of a projected room decoration on the theme of education and knowledge. In her simplicity, Sérusier's reader evokes the attitude of an antique scribe. The work's austere coloration is based on the gray that would come to dominate his palette, and the overall composition echoes Gauguin's Breton period. Although meeting Gauguin was like a revelation for Sérusier, he soon explored his own ideas and his own color scheme: In contrast to the wide range of pure and mixed colors Sérusier had employed under Gauguin's influence, he now became fascinated by the harmonious effect of a limited number of colors with the predominance of gray, some red, greenish-gray, white, and black. This palette enabled him to obtain the effect of tranquility he sought. The image as a whole, although peaceful, is not necessarily one of ease. The oversized book seems to weigh heavily on the girl, not only physically but also psychologically, hinting at the struggle of girls from rural areas to catch up on education and knowledge.

From comfortable middle-class origins, the extremely philosophical Sérusier went to school at the Lycée Condorcet, which produced many leaders of the French intellectual establishment. He founded the Nabis in 1889, whose members were in fact temperamentally very different from one another. The mystical and philosophical ones included Sérusier and Denis who were drawn especially towards the revival of sacred art. Bonnard and Vuillard, on the other hand, were not mystics; the ancient Breton culture did not appeal to them as subject matter. They were drawn instead to the fashionable Symbolist milieu including the elegant ladies inhabiting some of those drawing rooms.

Contemporary Muses

Maurice Denis (1870–1943)
Les Muses, 1893
Musée d'Orsay, Paris

Maurice Denis' group of young women reading is an updated interpretation of a motif from classical mythology: the muses of the arts and sciences. The nine muses are in contemporary dress and coiffure, and Denis also denies them the traditional attributes by which they might be recognized. One of the women in the foreground is Marthe whom the artist married in 1893 and who remained an inspiration to him until his death. Marthe is actually depicted twice: in the red dress in profile and from behind on the chair. The scene is set on the terrace of Saint-Germain-en-Laye, where Maurice Denis lived for his entire life. The chestnut trees are an important compositional element that emphasize the scene's tranquility and refer to Puvis de Chavannes' celebrated "sacred forest," evoking the rituals and prophesies of the "femmes visionaries." Equally mythological in subject and also set among tress (although in an orchard) are the reading women in Maurice Denis's painting *Wise Virgins* of 1893.

Maurice Denis was a leader of the Nabis (the Hebrew word for prophets), a group of artists who exhibited and worked together from 1891 to 1900. Their common style drew artistically from Gauguin's flat pattern compositions of the Brittany period (for example *La Vision du sermon* of 1888) as well the mythological subjects of Puvis de Chavannes. Book illustration and lithography were favored artistic vehicles of the group, as well as posters and theatre decoration.

The Artist's Daughter

Théophile van Rysselberghe (1862–1926)
Portrait of Jeanne Pissarrro, ca. 1895
The Museum of Fine Arts, Houston

The year 1895 saw an intensification of the artist's friendship with Camille Pissarro and on Rysselberghe's visit to France the artist began this portrait of Jeanne, Pissarro's fourteen-year-old daughter. Jeanne wanted to follow in her father's footsteps as a painter and frequently visited museums and artist's studios together with him. Whereas Camille Pissarro was supportive of his daughter's ambitions, her mother Julie was far less enthusiastic and disparaged the idea whenever possible; the girl's dream of becoming an artist thus fell victim to traditional roles, namely those of wife and mother.

"As a Pointillist painter, Théophile van Rysselberghe was the only artist who placed great importance on portraiture. His portraits were highly regarded for maintaining the human qualities of his models in spite of his use of Georges Seurat's Pointillist technique." Born in Ghent, he first studied at its Académie des Beaux-Arts, and later at the Académie in Brussels; he was one of the prominent co-founders of the Belgian artistic circle Les Vingt (The Twenty) in 1883 with such notable avant-garde artists as James Ensor, Fernand Khnopff, and later Auguste Rodin and Paul Signac.

The Nostalgic Reader

Cecilia Beaux (1855–1942)
New England Woman, 1895
Courtesy of the Pennsylvania Academy of the Fine Arts, Philadelphia

Detail
Time stands still for a quiet moment of reflection upon the past.

Caught in a pensive mood, the sitter has paused from reading what seems to be a journal or important leaflet; two books on the table are waiting to be read. The painting demonstrates both the "artist's facility with her figures" and a nostalgic atmosphere. The sitter's period costume, obviously a morning gown since the painting is set in her cousin's bedroom, "evokes the idea of colonial America." This kind of nostalgia for the country's past was fashionable at the turn of the century, however Beaux expresses it with the most modern of painterly means. The depiction of family members—in this case Mrs. Jedediah H. Richards, Cecilia Beaux's second cousin Julia Leavitt (1840–1915)—gave the artist the freedom to experiment artistically in familiar and intimate settings.

The prolific Cecilia Beaux grew up in the care of her maternal grandmother and aunt in Philadelphia who encouraged her talent. By the standards of her time, Beaux was a modern woman: She was free-spirited and devoted her entire energy and time to painting. She followed her art to shows in Paris and New York and repeatedly fell in love with younger men, yet never married. In addition to family members, her sitters came from the East Coast high society, including such luminaries as Theodore Roosevelt, Mrs. Andrew Carnegie, and the eminent writer Henry James. Her selective acquisition of sitters (Beaux's opinion was that "It doesn't pay to paint everybody") earned her a reputation as a "business-wise artist." In her summer home Green Alley at Gloucester, run in the fashion of a Salon, Beaux treated her friends from the highest social and intellectual circles of Boston and its environs to readings, theatricals, and other cultural events.

Cecilia Beaux

GUSTAV
KLIMT

The Secret Notebook

Gustav Klimt (1862–1918)
Portrait of Sonja Knips,
1898
Austrian Gallery Belvedere,
Vienna

Sonja Knips (1873–1959) epitomized the type of woman who captured Klimt's fascination. Very beautiful and born into an aristocratic family, Knips enjoyed considerable influence in Vienna's cultural and social life and was particularly involved in the activities of the Wiener Werkstätte. Although a truly modern women of fin de siècle Vienna, she delicately balanced her public persona between conformity and self-determination, thus stepping outside women's traditional role without creating a scandal.

The red book in her hand is a notebook, actually a very special one, for it is an important puzzle piece in the story of the relationship between the sitter and the artist. Recent research has revealed that Sonja gave the notebook to Klimt as a gift, who in turn filled it with sketches and returned it to her. She kept it all her life and added a tiny photograph of the artist, hinting at a romance between the two. This assumption is further supported by an unusual fan found in Sonja's estate, which Klimt had painted and on which he wrote a Persian poem as well as a quote from Goethe's "Claudine von Billa Bella." Since the poem unmistakably expresses Klimt's non-committal attitude towards their relationship, the fan can also be interpreted as a farewell letter. A year later, in 1896, Sonja married an industrialist, a marriage viewed by some of her friends as one of convenience.

Despite avant-garde elements, Klimt adhered to an aesthetic standard in which the idea of truth was closely connected to that of beauty—the nature of his art lies in the search for beauty in all forms.

Embracing the Young Reader

Mary Cassatt (1844–1926)
Family Group Reading,
ca. 1901
Philadelphia Museum of Art

Born into an affluent Philadelphia family, Mary Cassatt intelligently circumvented biased altitudes towards female artists by concentrating on scenes of domestic life. Many of her paintings describe the boundless love between mother and child, and she conveys this intimacy with eloquent simplicity; the artist dearly loved children. The setting of *Family Group Reading* resembles the area around the pond at Beaufresne, her home near Paris. Flanked by two adults, the child forms the center of the group, stressing her psychological and narrative importance and the responsibilities of the female family members as caretakers and as tutors.

Cassatt began her studies at the Pennsylvania Academy of Fine Art in Philadelphia but was soon disillusioned with the chauvinistic attitude of her male colleagues. When her father finally agreed to her wish to become a professional artist and further her studies in Paris, where she arrived in 1866, she took instruction from the renowned private teacher Jean-Léon Gérôme (the Ècole des Beaux-Arts did not yet admit women). Family members accompanied her to France and served as live-in chaperons with a watchful eye to any possible exposure to dangerous influences such as feminists ideas and Bohemian behavior: She was, for example, not allowed to frequent the cafes of the avant-garde, but her family eventually came to accept colleagues such as Degas, Morisot, and Caillebotte, since they all came from respectable families.

Mary Cassatt was the only American who wholeheartedly embraced the Impressionist style in the mid 1870s, and she exhibited with the Impressionists from 1879 onwards. Her mentor Edgar Degas inspired her interest in figural composition. Although living abroad, Cassatt played an important role at home; she exhibited frequently in the United States and advised important wealthy Americans such as Louisine and H. O. Havemeyer in their collecting activities.

Carefree Relaxation

Emanuel Phillips Fox
(1865–1915)
A Love Story, 1903
City of Ballarat Fine Art
Gallery, Ballarat, Victoria

Based on an earlier version painted in 1901 for which one of his students Ursula Foster was the model, the painting shows an elegantly dressed young lady reading a novel in a hammock in the shade of a tree on a summer's day. With its restricted palette and liberal use of white and broken brushwork, Phillips Fox has created an image of reading as carefree relaxation.

One of three paintings exhibited by Fox when he made his debut at the Royal Academy London in 1903, *A Love Story* was considered to be one of the most truthful representations of atmosphere and light in the exhibition. The Australian Fox, who spent much of his working life in England and France, developed a style that epitomizes the opulent era marked by the reign of King Edward VII. A student of the National Gallery School, Melbourne (1878–1886), Fox went to France in 1887 where he studied at the École des Beaux Arts and spent some time with plein air artists in France and England before returning to establish an art school in Melbourne with Tudor St. George in 1893, the most vital art school in Melbourne in the 1890s.

The Wholesome American Girl

Edmund Charles Tarbell
(1862–1938)
Josephine and Mercie, 1908
In the Collection of
The Corcoran Gallery of Art

Josephine and Mercie, the artist's two eldest daughters, are doing what society now expected from a cultivated girl: studying. Mercie is deeply absorbed in her book while Josephine studies at her desk. The girls would have had the best education available at the time, although not one aimed at a professional activity. The most appropriate career for a young woman was still that of mother and wife.

The representation is a visual transcription of the "wholesome American girl": the white dresses symbolize innocence and naturalness and the girls' activity embodies cultural refinement. The "wholesome American girl" represented the ideal of young womanhood: unaffected, innocent, civilized, intelligent, and studious. In both the figures and the furnishings, this early-twentieth-century interior scene also epitomizes the cult of domestic life and is steeped in conservative New England tradition and values.

The "poet of domesticity," Tarbell, son of an old New England family, regularly used family members as models. At the time of this painting he taught at the School of the Museum of Fine Arts in Boston and was famous for the interior scenes painted in his summer home in New Castle, New Hampshire (*Girl Reading, A Girl Crocheting,* and *New England Interior*); *Josephine and Mercie* was also painted there. The Boston Sunday Herald of 1908 hailed *Josephine and Mercie* as "the best picture of the year." The artist's ambitious outdoor scenes such as *In the Orchard, Breakfast on the Piazza,* and *Mother and Child in a Boat* reflect contemporary American values no less than his interiors.

PAXTON
1910

Forbidden Fruit

William McGregor Paxton
(1869–1941)
The House Maid, 1910
In the Collection of
The Corcoran Gallery of Art

The liveried maid with a telltale feather duster tucked under one arm seems to be lost in the pages of a book rather than working. Perhaps she is just a working-class young woman seeking to educate herself whenever the opportunity arises, even if this means neglecting her work and browsing through her employer's books. But she could also be one of those "wayward housemaids" much feared by Boston's leisure-class ladies: Not only does she intently scan the book, but she also stands before an open file box most likely containing personal and private information about her employer's guests and friends. Leaks of private information were of great concern for they could lead to grave consequences, even extortion, as described, for example, in Edith Wharton's 1905 *House of Mirth* where an observant charwomen blackmails the aspiring socialite Lily Bart.

Born in Baltimore, the accomplished Paxton completed his studies with Joseph DeCamp at Cowles Art School, where he met his wife Elisabeth Okie, who also studied there. Some of Paxton's favorite artists were Velasquez and Vermeer; the influence of the latter is clearly visible in the present composition. The young maid is an attractive, even sensuous figure, beautifully complementing the still life of fine Chinese ginger jars and a small Japanese figurine on the table.

Like his contemporary Tarbell, Paxton was a member of the Boston School, among whose artists a female figure in a moment of solitary reflection was a favorite subject; Paxton, however, was its only member to depict servants as solitary figures. His motivation behind the *House Maid* could be the simple beauty of the figure and her setting, but the work might also contain a social statement that thematizes differences in privilege, or even amount to a provocation aimed at overly suspicious employers of Boston's high society.

Painted Diaries

John Singer Sargent
(1856–1925)
Simplon Pass: Reading, 1911
Museum of Fine Arts Boston
The Hayden Collection

The figures depicted in *Simplon Pass* in the Swiss Alps are the painter's sister Emily Sargent, herself an accomplished painter, and her daughter Rose-Marie Ormond. The cosmopolitan Sargents were avid travelers and while other people may have written diaries, Sargent painted his. Whether in Palestine, the Dolomites, Corfu, Italy, Spain, Portugal, Turkey, Norway, Greece, Egypt, France, or the Balearic Islands—with his family and often an entire entourage—Sargent recorded these trips in his work. His pictorial diary of their visit to Simplon Pass in 1911 includes such truly remarkable works as *The Tease* and *The Lesson*.

Sargent's watercolors are among his greatest achievements and "are freer, more experimental and more personal than most of his works in oil." Women and their books are a recurring subject in his paintings, as for example in *The Misses Vickers* of 1884 (Sheffield Galleries and Museum Trust), *Mrs Carl Meyer and her Children* of 1896 (private collection), and *Hylda, Daughter of Asher and Mrs. Wertheimer* of 1905 (Tate Gallery, London), in which Hylda sets her book down on the table behind her while her attention is drawn by something happening on the floor—perhaps she is looking down at a playing child.

Born in Florence to an expatriate American family and trained in Paris, the cosmopolitan Sargent, who had every opportunity to participate in the experiments of the French avant-garde, was first exposed to art by his mother, a capable watercolorist. He never embraced the avant-garde style, but remained "between traditionalism and modernism, yet committed to neither."

Enchanting Moments

Sir James Jebusa Shannon
(1862–1923)
In the Dunes, ca. 1910
Smithsonian American Art Museum, Washington, D.C.

Lady Shannon and their only daughter Kitty, both in cosmopolitan finery, enjoy an enchanting moment reading together at the seaside of Egmond, a thriving beach resort. The image is a lovely example of reading shared between two generations. Egmond, where Jacob van Ruisdael had already frequently painted in the seventeenth century, consists of a cluster of three very small villages on the North Sea coast of the Netherlands. In the 1880s, the American artists Julius Garibaldi Melchers and George Hitchcock founded an artist's colony at the site, The American Painters Club. By 1900 Egmond had formed a tourist association to develop the town's potential.

Shannon, an American-born expatriate who settled in London, studied under Sir Edward Poynter in 1878 and although he always intended to return to America, the success of his beautiful portraits of society and aristocratic ladies, including commissions from Queen Victoria in the years 1881–82, prompted him to stay. His wife and daughter were his favorite models and other enchanting scenes of reading include *Jungle Tales* of 1895 in which a mother reads to her two daughters (Metropolitan Museum of Art, New York) and *Mother and Child* (private collection) of around 1900–10, in which his daughter Kitty is leaning against her mother's lap and daydreaming while Lady Shannon reads. In 1922, Shannon renounced his U.S. citizenship in order to accept the knighthood he was awarded in recognition of his talent as a portrait artist.

“Some Books
Are to Be
Tasted, Others
To Be
Swallowed, and
Some Few
To Be Chewed
and Digested”

FRANCIS BACON, *OF STUDIES*

Reading Becomes Art: The Twentieth Century

In the twentieth century, the subject matter of women reading is embedded in the innovations of various artistic movements. Compared to late-nineteenth-century paintings, these images frequently exhibit an emotional detachment from their sitters, who have become first and foremost vehicles for intellectual analysis and artistic experimentation. Moreover, the female figure in these images represents the collective or universal rather than individual reader. Only in exceptional cases, such as the paintings by August Macke or Gino Severini discussed here (pages 186, 190), are the sitters specific individuals and identified as such in the painting's title.

With Western society's growing acceptance of female individualism, it became impossible to restrict women's access to the full spectrum of literature. Women now commanded their own authority over books, as writers and readers; the patriarchs had all but surrendered in their attempt to withhold books. Whereas in the past owning books, let alone collecting them, had been reserved for a narrow segment of society, the twentieth-century's growing material abundance enabled people from all walks of life, and in particular women, to take pleasure in surrounding themselves with books.

Accordingly, twentieth and twenty-first-century images depict the act of reading in a modern language that departs from the enchanting and fleeting moments of the nineteenth century, in which reading was primarily a leisure activity. Reading by women is no longer redolent of something overly refined or ceremonious, but has become part of their everyday lives. Moreover, by the end of the century, the act of reading has become increasingly associated with women; today more books are read by women than by men.

Indeed, women's connection with books was no longer a sensation, or even a novelty; the relation between a woman's choice of reading material and her behavior was of little relevance. The subject matter of women reading no longer carried associations of something forbidden, illicit, or unusual, and as a result it no longer piqued the interest of avant-garde artists. Leisure time as well has assumed a new meaning in the twentieth century; it is no longer considered a privilege but, as expressed by Ferdinand Léger, for example, a right earned by the working man (page 188).

At the turn of the twentieth century, however, the so-called new or modern woman (not necessarily flattering terms) was still something of an outsider. The appearance of a newspaper in the hands of a woman, for example, was a potent symbol of modernity. Although women had conquered the stage as equal participants in everything cultural by now—indeed men feared a "feminization" of culture—newspapers, which quintessentially represented their readers' connection to the world of commerce and politics, were not the most feminine reading material. Paintings of women reading newspapers are few—it is the socio-political cartoons in the newspapers that present this activity mockingly.

The history of the visual arts in the twentieth century is a constant re-evaluation of pictorial ideas and a rapid succession of -isms and movements, but this is only one explanation for the greatly varied stylistic vocabulary in paintings of women reading. These images now embody an aesthetic and formal development that is primarily concerned with what art is and what it can or should do. Depictions of women reading are now, like any other images, vehicles for these artistic explorations; they examine issues of social progress, emotion, alienation: universally human themes rather than the character or qualities of a specific sitter

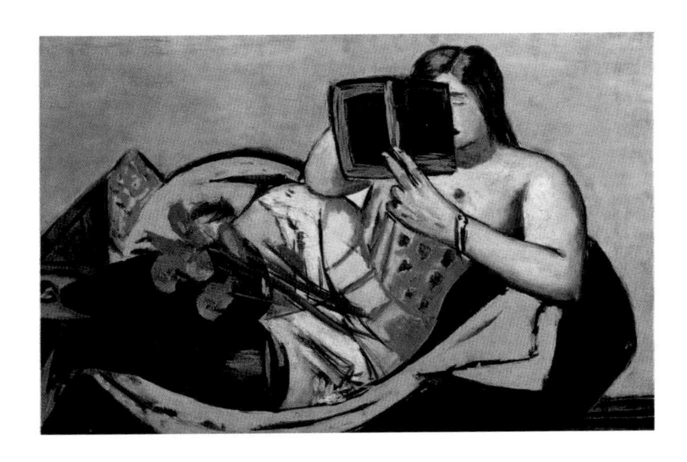

1 Max Beckmann (1884–1950)
Reclining Woman with Book and Irises, 1931
Austrian Galerie Belvedere, Vienna

Beckmann's reader is direct and elusive at the same time. It is not clear what the woman reads or who she is; to judge by her dress, she might be a member of the demimonde. Two years after this painting, Beckmann's personal odyssey as a victim of the Nazi regime began: in 1933 he lost his teaching job of eighteen years at the Frankfurt academy. He subsequently moved to Berlin and settled in Amsterdam in 1937, leaving Europe for the United States in 1947.

or subject as an individual. The sitter has become a means to a larger and more universal end. Furthermore, these images embody an unprecedented, even democratic, openness in their depiction of subjects from every social class.

Women's association with the interior, with the home, has shed its restrictive aspect in twentieth-century works too; the woman is no longer relegated to an interior associated solely with domestic responsibilities, but the home she inhabits is now a treasured private sphere, and the works of art discussed here embody a new respect for women's roles within this world. The German Expressionist, August Macke depicts his wife, for example, beautifully framed by this private world, in which her self-possessed figure is entirely and serenely at home (page 186). Its style perhaps belies its ostensibly conservative subject matter, but it nonetheless represents reading not as an elite privilege, but a natural part of women's domestic lives.

His reading woman is the madam of the establishment. Munch, who continuously battled emotional instability and its subsequent excesses said, "My life has always been along the abyss," and in his art sought "to show men who breathe, feel, love and suffer." He was friends with several great contemporary writers, such as the Swedish dramatist Strindberg, who shared his gloomy philosophy on existential questions and sexual relationships. He was also in contact with the Danish philosopher Soren Kierkegaard, and with Fyodor Dostojevsky, whose great novels not only transformed the late-nineteenth-century European sensibility but continue to profoundly affect any sensitive reader.

In *Le Grand Déjeuner,* the optimistic Ferdinand Léger paints his vision of a new and socially just society; many of his paintings take the modern working class as their subject (page 188). Léger saw leisure time (to which reading

2 Gerhard Richter (b. 1932)
Lesende (Reading), 1994
San Francisco Museum of Modern Art

One of Gerhard Richter's photo-paintings, in this work the sitter bending her head to read is the wife of the artist; its composition and light effects recall the intimate portraits of Vermeer from the seventeenth century. But Richter has created a contemporary image: "The reader wears a scrunchee in her hair and is reading a copy of 'Der Spiegel,' a weekly German newsmagazine."Der Spiegel,' a weekly German newsmagazine."

In comparison, Isaac Israels' *Women Reading* of 1903 is more provocative and challenging (page 182). Devoid of any clear reference to setting, and certainly a far remove from Macke's domestic space, Israel's subject sits upright (even defiantly) and smokes while she reads. She is quite clearly a "modern woman," who openly demonstrates her independence. While in 1903 such an image of a woman reading and smoking may still have possessed something scandalous, even shocking, later in the century it is increasingly the formal innovations, rather than the subject matter, that have assumed this role.

Around the same time as Israel's image, Edvard Munch, who keenly felt the emotional tension that modern society inflicted upon the individual, celebrated Christmas at a brothel (page 184) and does not hesitate to include himself in the painting in a lamentable stage of drunkenness.

intrinsically belonged) not as the prerogative of the "leisure class," but the just reward of the working man (or woman). *Le Grand Déjeuner*, regarded as one of his three or four greatest pictures, is a social as well as an art historical statement. It depicts an ideal social order, and is at the same time a pictorial resumé of great artistic themes from the past such as the nude, the odalisque, or the three graces, as well making reference to sculpture.

One of the indisputably greatest artists of Modernism, Henri Matisse (page 196), saw reading as a metaphor for painting, a privileged form of access to the world, and the expression of an inner wealth of experience. Reading comes to symbolize an inner world, into which the viewer is invited to participate but simultaneously excluded from. A painting, in the words of the artist, is "like a book on the shelf of a bookcase, showing only the few words of its title, which needs, to give up its riches, the action of the reader who must take it up, open it, and shut himself away with it."

Artists of the early-twenty-first century face an interesting choice between continuing to push the boundaries of artistic expression into new directions in their search for individual self-expression by exploring the extreme, the radical, or the cutting-edge, and instead pursuing a more classical orientation, characterized by universality, craftsmanship, restraint, clarity, and idealism. The contemporary artists included here make this choice informed by the richness of their own aesthetic language; their work exists in a continuum that has always helped to define humanity. With regard to the subject matter of reading in general (and women reading in particular) they also promote cultural ideas of literacy as a reminder that reading is a social ingredient of our existence.

Intrinsically connected to his African American heritage, Lovell's tableaux, for example, are historical records of people who have not been memorialized (page 205). The title of *Salvation* refers to an entire historical process; by encapsulating this process within the subject matter of an African-American woman reading Lovell calls attention to reading itself as both advantage and deliverance. For both Patricia Watwood and Glass equally (pages 206, 208), creating a scene of a woman reading is an acknowledgement of the fact that cultural pursuits help define civilization. In this, the act of reading by a woman and painting by an artist are one and the same, in their broadest meaning both are expressions of humanity and civilization.

At a time when reading by women has become self-evident, the images in this volume serve as reminders of the long distance from the few aristocratic women who presented their books to the viewer as symbols of their piety or elite status to the self-evident and informal nature of reading for the modern woman. Whereas at the beginning of this journey, access to and choice of reading material were determined solely by a woman's social status—and female literacy was an exception in any case—after overcoming centuries of social restraints, prejudice, and paternalistic surveillance, reading has finally become a limitlessly varied and democratic activity.

3 Semon Afanasevich Chuikov (1902–1980)
The Daughter of Soviet Kirghizia, 1950
Private Collection
Courtesy Overland Gallery

Chuikov, who had to fend for himself from the age of twelve, labored hard during summer and attended school in winter. A graduate of the Odessa Art School, he earned a place at the Turkestan regional art school in Tashkent in 1920. In the early 1930s he set up a Kirghizia artist's union and repeatedly served as its chairman between 1934 and 1943. The *Daughter of Soviet Kirghizia* expresses Chuikov's love for his country as well as the Soviet Union's pride in its educational standards even in the remotest places of her country.

The "New Woman"

Isaac Israels (1865–1934)
Woman Reading,
ca. 1903–07
Collection Kröller-Müller Museum, Otterlo

The son of Hague School painter Jozef Israels, Isaac Isreals was attracted to the exciting nightlife and demimonde of his hometown of Amsterdam, and later of Paris and London, between which he divided his time between 1903 and 1923. He loved to depict women putting on their make-up, dining alone in restaurants, or sitting on a bench in de Bois de Bologne with a stack of books next to them and reading the newspaper. Among these paintings of modern and independent women is a fabulous full-length portrait of the legendary spy Mata Hari painted in 1916 and now in the collection of the Kröller-Müller Museum.

The identity of the sitter of the present painting is not known but, flamboyantly dressed and smoking, she was certainly the kind of modern woman whom Isreals would have met in one of the literary cafes or during his nightly tours. Despite depicting his sitters as very self-determined women, he renders them impressionistically, which not only softens the potential radicalism of their activities, but also presents their independence as something completely natural. The numerous paintings of women reading in Isreals' oeuvre might be linked to his own great interest in literature, which he had developed already as a child.

The Demimonde

Edvard Munch (1863–1944)
Christmas in the Brothel,
1903–04
Munch Museum, Oslo

Like other painters such as Toulouse-Lautrec, the Norwegian artist Edvard Munch drew inspiration for his work from the extraordinary atmosphere of the world of the demimonde. In the weeks before Christmas of 1903, Munch was working on a commission in Lübeck; tensions between the artist and his patron had been mounting, and the fact that Munch spent Christmas at a brothel increased them. Consequently, Munch's difficult psychological disposition was getting worse, as was his excessive alcohol consumption.

In the present painting Munch includes himself crouching on a bench in the back of the painting, obviously sleeping off his drunkenness. Whether or not he sought other personal comfort at such an establishment can only be speculated. Whereas the overall mood of the painting is melancholic, it is not entirely gloomy. The madam of the establishment, dressed in her best decent clothes—as are her girls in the background—is smoking and reading. The book she reads may well be a Christmas story since her facial expression radiates a kind of joyful interest, an indication that the painting is not an unholy version of a Christmas night.

The undisputed pioneer of the Expressionist movement, Edvard Munch wanted to paint pictures expressive of states of mind: he took as his subject matter love, hate, life and death, illness, and the pain of loneliness.

Munch's oeuvre must be understood against the background of his dramatic personal experiences of sickness and death within his family, his own fragile disposition, and his dramatic and unhappy love affairs. He was just five years old when his mother died at the early age of thirty; the death of his favorite sister followed in 1877: she was just fifteen. In 1889 he had to bury his father; his sister Laura was in permanent treatment for depression. Of the five siblings only Andreas ever married, to die a few month later.

The Perfect Model

August Macke (1887–1914)
Wife of the Artist (study for a portrait), 1912
Staatliches Museum Preußischer Kulturbesitz, Nationalgalerie Berlin

August Macke married Elisabeth Gerhard in 1909. She brought with her a substantial dowry, affording the couple a carefree existence. From the beginning of their marriage onwards she was his favorite model, as he himself explained, "I do not need to work with women who do not command natural harmonic movements and who need constant instructions for posing." Macke was particularly fond of depicting his beloved wife, for him the embodiment of femininity, during the activity of reading or even knitting. Elisabeth had an intense interest in literature and actually had literary aspirations herself, which however, did not bear fruit.

The present painting is obviously an evening scene; a lamp glows behind the seated Elisabeth, who reads in a pose of concentration and serenity at the same time. She assumes a similar, naturally relaxed pose while reading in *Elisabeth at the Desk* of 1911, and both works display Macke's brilliant fauvist style, in which color carries the motif, and his mastery at reducing the pictorial elements to the essentials.

A founding member (together with Wassily Kandinsky and Franz Marc) of the Blaue Reiter in 1911, Macke maintained a close contact with his artist colleagues in Paris, where he found great inspiration. His visit, together with Marc, to Robert Delaunay in Paris in 1912 as well as his journey to Tunis in 1914 with Paul Klee were decisive factors in the emergence of his mature style, a synthesis of Cubism and Fauvism.

Among the first soldiers drafted into service in France at the outbreak of World War I, Macke was killed only a few weeks later, in September of 1914 at the age of twenty-seven. Franz Marc was soon to follow, in 1916. Elisabeth remarried after Macke's untimely death, at which time their only son was four years old. Reminiscing on their work together she said, "I have particularly lovely memories of these sessions, it gave me the feeling of belonging to his work."

Well-Earned Leisure

Fernand Léger (1881–1955)
Le Grand Déjeuner, 1921
The Museum of Modern Art, New York

Detail
The book now belongs to women's everyday world.

For Ferdinand Léger, leisure, as depicted in *Le Grand Déjeuner*—where women are having breakfast and a seated figure is reading—was not a frivolous escape from modern life, but something "earned by modern man. Leger was an optimist who believed that modern technology would release man from drudgery. This is why even in the factory pictures of 1917 to 1920 he seldom showed men actually working: They usually stand or sit, nearly inactive because man, with his promethean abilities, has produced machinery that does the work for him." *Le Grand Déjeuner* occupies a logical place within Leger's explication of the ideal society. His nudes of 1920 began to use women as symbols of release from labor, or even as symbols of the reward for labor. *Le Grand Déjeuner* is the central masterpiece of this period in which women are identified with leisure. His men, in contrast, are placed in factories and tugboats; their domain is the street or the wharf. Women are absent from these images, for their realm is the interior.

The book in Léger's painting is not a compositional element but an expression of the female world. His oeuvre includes a large group of monumental female figures with books such as *Les Odalisques* of 1920, *La Tasse de thé*, *La femme au chat*, *Femme au bouquet*, and *Femme dans un intérieur*, as well as two versions of *Le Petit Déjeuner*, all from 1921.

Born in the Norman city of Argentan, Léger developed his distinctive style from rendering three-dimensional units resembling segments of cones, cylinders, and other solids in 1914. Around 1920 his pictorial aesthetic departed from the "mechanical period"; objects and figures are now comprehended more organically, although influences from the *mechanica* are still visible.

The Bookbinder

Gino Severini (1883–1966)
Portrait of Gina Severini (My Daughter), 1934
Galeria Civica d'arte Moderna e Contemporanea, Turin

The book the artist's daughter Gina holds is an acknowledgment of her professional skills as a bookbinder, much admired by her father. In the early thirties Severini, a student of Giacomo Balla, shared much of his time with the so-called Paris Italians such as Giorgio De Chirico, Renato Paresce, Massimo Campigli and others, who argued in favor of a painting style inspired by antiquity and spoke explicitly of a "return to craftsmanship." Consequently, Severini's portraits of the time, some of which he showed at the Rome Quadrennial in 1935, have a classical Roman feel.

A leading member of the Futurist movement, Severini lived in Paris from 1906 and was an important link between artists in France and Italy. He was instrumental in organizing Futurist exhibitions outside Italy, for example in Paris, London, Berlin, and the United States. Severini abandoned Futurism, which was not only an artistic but also a literary movement, around 1920. He also turned his back on the Synthetic Cubism with which he had briefly experimented in favor of theories of classical balance based on figurative subjects drawn from the traditional commedia dell'arte. In the 1950s, he returned to the subject matter of his Futurist years. Born in Cortona, Italy, Severini published important theoretical essays and books on art throughout his career.

G.Severin

Intimate Moments

Pablo Picasso (1881–1973)
Femme Lisant, 1935
Musée Picasso, Paris

From the mid 1930s Picasso's pictorial language becomes more expressive and radical. Within this radicalism is an artistic freedom that disregards any obligatory style. His visual vocabulary comprises stylized spatial disruptions, deformations of natural form, and sweeping coloristic choices. At the time (1931–34), he was also collaborating with Julio Gonzáles on sculptures and was attracted to the problems being tackled by the Surrealists.

The sitter is Marie-Thérèse Walter (1909–1977), whom Picasso met in 1927 when she was just seventeen years young, and who inspired Picasso with her grace, beauty, and youthful vitality. Married to Olga Khokhlova, a ballerina of Diaghilev's Ballets Russes, Picasso kept the affair secret until Marie-Thérèse became pregnant with Maya in 1935. Picasso did not divorce Olga, for he did not want to give her half his wealth, to which she would have been entitled according to French law. Marie-Thérèse was literally replaced by Dora Maar in 1936–37; heartbroken, she never recovered from the ill treatment she received from Picasso and four years after his death she took her own life.

Picasso started a series of reading women around May 1934, often with one or two figures reading at a table. The "reader" in Picasso's oeuvre can be linked to the sweet and fragile Marie-Thérèse Walter, for after their child Maya was born, Picasso stopped portraying the intimate act of reading; from now on books appear only in his still lifes.

Picasso, together with Matisse, is one of the undisputed geniuses of the twentieth century. Less well known is that the titan Picasso also wrote some fascinating poetry in the format of a diary between the years of 1935 and 1959.

The Vulnerable Reader

Yasuo Kuniyoshi
(1889–1943)
I'm Tired, 1938
Whitney Museum of
American Art, New York

Kuniyoshi's depictions of single female figures are meant to portray a collective rather than an individual women, a woman representing all women. His models are melancholic and pensive, with an air of inwardness and female vulnerability. "It seems of greater value to paint my conception of a woman; to express my inner feelings toward the [subject] is more important than the physical aspects of any individual . . . The importance and impact lie in grasping the content of the matter, the essence pulsating within itself. Instead of painting from the outside in, my efforts have been to concentrate on inside out." *I'm Tired* typifies this intimate viewpoint. The model rests, leaning against an open copy of the *Daily* as if reflecting on the text. The presence of the newspaper and the melancholic mood of the woman are also an expression of Kuniyoshi's overwhelming and painful concern with the worldwide political events looming at the time (the period of World War II was probably the most difficult time of his life).

Born in Japan into a modest Okayama family, Kuniyoshi came to America in 1906 and arrived in New York (via Seattle and Los Angeles) in 1910. He studied art at the National Academy and the Art Students League, where he himself began to teach in 1933 and remained a popular teacher for the next twenty years. From the 1930s on, Kuniyoshi's work figured prominently in important national exhibitions of American art; he has also been the recipient of numerous art prizes. The originality of his work lies in its successful fusion of the oriental and occidental.

Henri Matisse 39

Hidden Abundance

Henri Matisse (1869–1954)
Reader on a Black Background, 1939
Musée National d'Art Moderne – Centre Georges Pompidou, Paris

The motif of the reading figure occurs in Matisse's oeuvre from very early on; like any other bourgeois household, his at the time was a conservative one, and it is primarily the female members who are pictured as readers in the surroundings of their home. *The Reader* of 1895 depicts his model Caroline Joblaud with whom he fathered a daughter, Marguerite, born in 1894. Marguerite, whom he repeatedly portrays throughout his career, is also the sitter in *Interior with a Young Girl Reading* of 1905–06, or *Marguerite, Reading* of 1906. In 1898 Matisse married Amélie Noellie Parayre; the couple raised Marguerite together with their two sons, Jean (born in 1899) and Pierre (born in 1900).

Matisse generally pictures his readers with downcast eyes, emphasizing their detachment from the outside world in favor of concentrating on a hidden abundance. This is particularly exemplified by *Le silence habité des maisons* of 1947, in which two women, without faces, concentrate on a large book. From June to September of 1939, Matisse stayed at the Hotel Lutétia in Paris and worked in a studio at the Villa Alésia lent to him by the American sculptor Mary Callery. The present painting was executed there, its sitter was the Hungarian model Wilma Javor. The work represents Matisse's sophisticated, severely simplified, and geometrically organized style.

Matisse's paintings celebrate the richness of life, and are the result of the highly intelligent artist's careful planning and calculation. The metaphor of the image is evoked in this work by the window frame, which becomes an expression of the creative process itself, by means of the mirror and the model's reflection in the mirror, which the artist has placed between the young woman and her schematized body in the drawing.

The Rascals

Balthus (1908–2001)
The Three Sisters, 1959–64
Private Collection

One of the great figural painters of the twentieth century, Balthus populates his paintings with girls, or young women, and cats. No adults are present to supervise their activities, and the young women are free to do as they wish: read, dream, crawl around the ground, or engage in misdeeds. The eroticism in these seemingly traditional subjects, painted in muted tones, caused a stir as early as 1934, at his first one-man show in Paris. The element of erotic provocation became more oblique in his work after 1955: "I used to want to shock," he once told a friend, "but now it bores me." The models in the present painting are Sylvia, Marie-Pierre, and Beatrice Colle, daughters of the artist's friends.

Between 1959 and 1965 Balthus painted several versions of *The Three Sisters*, of which the present is most likely the best. The girl on the left and the girl kneeling on the ground are formally connected by the activity of reading and by the book, whereas the central figure appears isolated.

Born into an artistic family that left Poland for Paris in 1903—his father was the noted art historian and painter Erich Klossowski and his mother, Elisabeth Dorothea, was a painter known as Baladine—the self-taught Balthus (Balthasar Klossowski) lived in various European cities. After his parents' separation in 1917, it was none other than the foremost German poet of the day, Rainer Maria Rilke (1875–1926), who became like a surrogate father to him. Rilke was also instrumental in the publication of *Mitsou* in 1921, a book of forty ink drawings in which the thirteen-year-old Balthus illustrated his adventures with a stray cat.

The versatile artist also excelled as a stage designer; in 1934–35 he found inspiration for an extensive series of drawings inspired by Emily Bronte's *Wuthering Heights*, a book he greatly admired for its haunting story, which resonated with his own, at times, haunting representations of the ambiguous and dark side of childhood.

ГРАФИК
ВСТРЕЧУ

Books for All

Pavel Fedorovich Shardakov (b. 1929)
Milkmaids, City of Volgograd, 1967
Courtesy of a Friend of the Springville Museum of Art, Utah

The *Milkmaids* expresses one of the few advantages of the communist system, namely that of total and equal access to education for all its citizens. Its sitters are gathered at a table strewn with a chaos of books and papers and a vase of flowers; a bare light bulb hangs from the ceiling. The figure on the right reads while the other two gaze directly out at the viewer. A departure from the strict tenets of Socialist Realism, Shardakov's work is not a glorification of the communist system, but contains more ambivalent and even puzzling elements. In fact, the time in which this painting was executed witnessed a "withering of communist ideology, and as a consequence, the adulteration and decay of the principles of socialist realism. Freed, to a large extent, from coercion, and no longer guided by a unified and coherent set of rules, painters begin to go their separate ways. To a greater extent than ever before in the history of socialist realism, the artist was able to express individual concerns ... [Shardakov's] satire and modernistic formalism ... would not have been deemed appropriate for official Soviet art prior to this time."

Like in any other country of the world, in the Soviet Union, the education of its citizen was inextricably linked with employment, the economy, and of course, with ideology. Whereas the literacy rate of women in imperial Russia, according to a 1897 census, was apparently under fifteen percent, this figure jumped to sixty-five percent by 1937 and, some two decades later, all women were completely literate.

Born in Perm, Russia, Shardakov studied at Sverdlovsk Art College from 1947 to 1952 and the Leningrad Higher Arts and Crafts College from 1952 to 1958. He was active in Perm for the next seven years and thereafter in Volgograd (Stalingrad).

The Modern Reader

Roy Lichtenstein
(1923–1997)
Nude Reading, 1994
Roy Lichtenstein Foundation, New York

Roy Lichtenstein's long career and large body of work includes paintings, sculpture, and prints, and has made him one of America's greatest exponents of Pop Art. His subjects are often banal objects of modern commercial and industrial America and the mass media, enlarged comics, parodies of famous paintings including those of Abstract Expressionism, as well as formalized landscapes. His enlargement and simplification of the objects he depicts has an alienating effect and are meant to inspire the viewer to see them anew.

Lichtenstein's artistic development is marked by his propensity for working in series or thematic groups; he started his series of female nudes in 1993, and it includes several reading figures. Executed in Ben-Day dots, the series was first exhibited in November and December of 1994 at the Leo Castelli Gallery, where he also had his first one-man show of comic-strip paintings in 1962, the exhibition that essentially launched his career.

Born into a middle-class family in New York, Lichtenstein studied at the School of Fine Arts at Ohio State University and painted his earliest proto-Pop work in 1956.

SALVATION
BLAKE'S POEMS AND PROPHECIES
In The Hudson

Personal History

Whitfield Lovell (b. 1959)
Salvation, 2001
Collection of Patricia and Donald Oresman

Next to his installations, an important part of Whitfield Lovell's work comprises tableaux constructed from freehand charcoal drawings on vintage wood (for example old planks from architectural salvage or other places) combined with found objects from garage sales or flea markets. These objects are assembled in an intuitive process to create three-dimensional assemblages that vary from piece to piece. In the present work a support, on which several old books are piled up, has been attached to the painting. The titles of the books are worn and hard to read but they include *In the Hudson...*, Blake's *Poems and Prophecies*, *Cpik Tet Moral*, *Deutsche Liebeslieder*, and *Salvation*. The latter may be the source of the painting's title, and could also be a reference to the benefits of reading.

Incorporated into these assemblages is a sense of personal history that reflect the artist's African-American heritage. Lovell's masterful renderings of African-American figures are based on photographs he first borrowed from his grandmother and later started to collect from the same places as his wood planks; they span the period from around 1900 to 1960. His work pays tribute to the passage of time and provides the lives of anonymous African-Americans with an identity and endows them with dignity. Lovell, whose mother's family was from South Carolina and his father's from Barbados, was born in 1959 and grew up in the Bronx. He graduated in 1981 from Cooper Union and traveled extensively in Europe and Africa. His work has been exhibited worldwide and acquired by museums such as The Metropolitan Museum of Art, the Whitney Museum of American Art, and the Seattle Art Museum. He is a 2007 MacArthur fellowship recipient.

Detail
Access to books and literacy has always been an essential aspect of personal freedom.

Metamorphosis

Patricia Watwood (b. 1971)
Music and Poetry, 2000
Collection Margaret and
Gregory Hedberg, New York

Music and Poetry draws inspiration from Titian's lute players and odalisques. The two figures are a study in contrast, the woman's flesh pale and glowing, the man's dark and muscled. Unlike the classical odalisque, these figures are both engaged and engaging. She reads (*Metamorphosis*), while he plays, and although together, each is in his or her own mental world. They are sensuous, but also relaxed and self-possessed—the mental and the physical are in balance. The subject may be classical, but Watwood's subtle reinterpretation of the figures shows a synthesis of the modern mind and a new idea of femininity and masculinity.

Born in St. Louis, Missouri, Patricia Watwood, who lives and works in New York, is an emerging artist who is part of the New York Realist movement. She completed a rigorous academic training in drawing and oil painting at the Water Street Atelier under Jacob Collins and earned her M. F. A. at New York Academy of Art, launched in 1980 and shortly thereafter actively supported by Andy Warhol. Watwood's subjects are primarily figures and portraits, and through the medium of the nude and the human face she seeks to connect the modern audience with the timeless mysteries of the human character and the resonance of the human spirit. Her bright, colourful palette infuses her painted world with luminosity and a modern air.

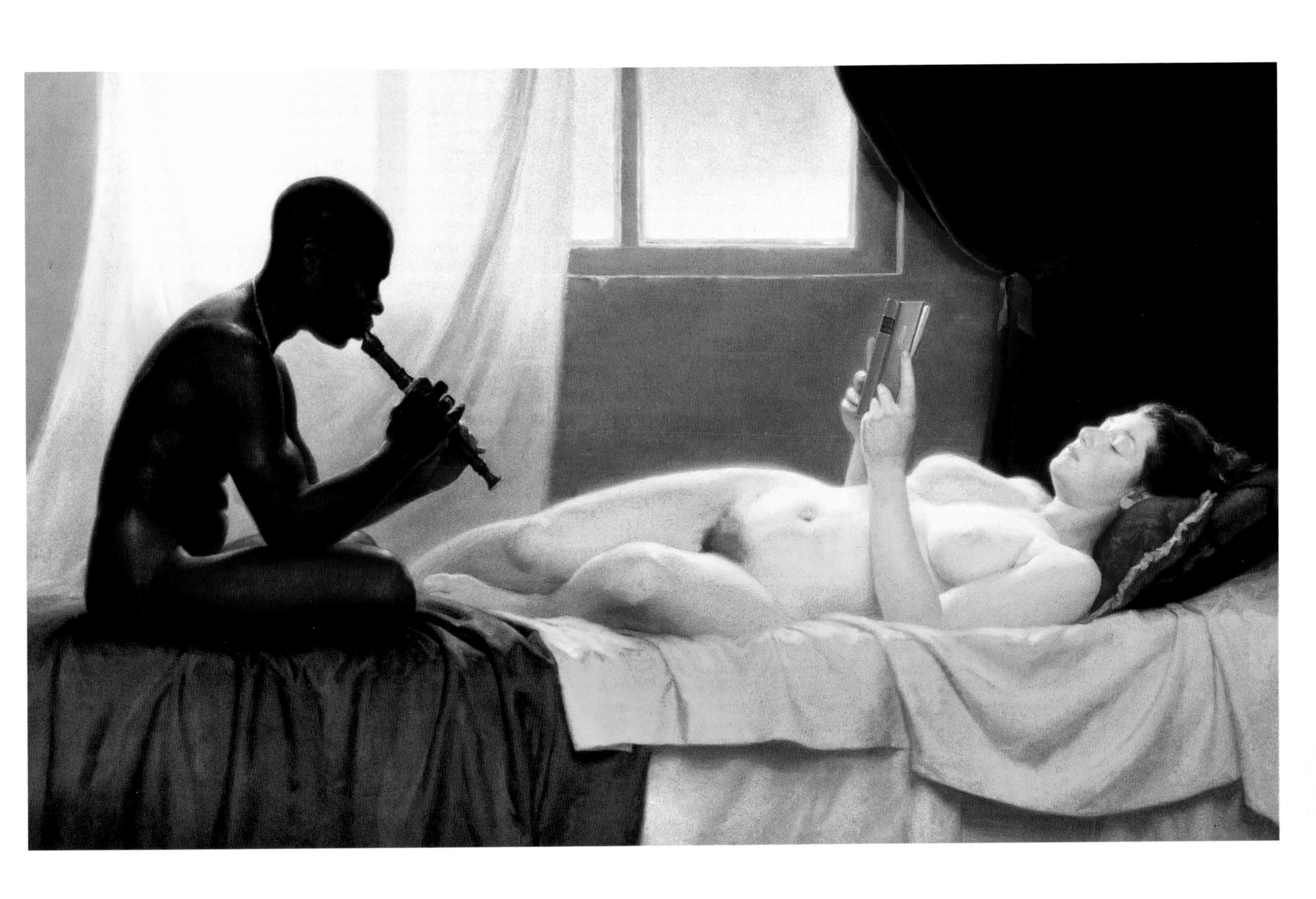

GLASS 03

A Break from Reading

Mikel Glass (b. 1962)
Elizabeth Shea, 2002
Collection of Dennis and Elizabeth Shea

This is not a photograph! Mikel Glass is one of the new Realist painters, whose impressively refined technique can shock with its beauty. The atmosphere created in the painting is like a powerful magnet, attracting the viewer so strongly that he can virtually feel and even hear the quiet breathing and relaxed heartbeat of a woman in her favorite environment, resting from the demanding schedule of a hard day's work. This is not only a portrait of Elizabeth Shea (a public relations executive), but life itself encapsulated in a precious moment of repose.

Born in Boston, Glass graduated from Pomona College and has an M. F. A. from the New York Academy of Art. Living in New Jersey and working in New York, Glass stresses that the driving philosophy behind his portraiture is that in order to be successful, a piece must work first as a painting and second as a commissioned portrait; in this work he has achieved precisely this, for who among his viewers would not wish to project themselves into the sitter's place? The thoroughly contemporary and honest feeling of this work was surprising even to some of the artist's more traditional fellow Realists.

Sources Cited

CHAPTER 1

Binkley, Roberta, *Biography of Enheduanna, Priestess of Inanna.* Available online at http://www.cddc.vt.edu/feminism/Enheduanna.html.
Cahill, Thomas, *How the Irish Saved Civilization* (London, 1995), 184.
Charity, Willard, *Christine de Pizan: Her Life and Works* (New York, 1984).
Encyclopedia Britannica's Guide to Women' History, 2006. Available online at http://www.britannica.com/women.
Hatz, Melanie J., *Art of the First Cities* (New York, 2003), 200.
Hinsch, Brett, *Women in Early Imperial China* (Lanham, Maryland, 2002), 116, 123.
http://search.eb.com/women/print?articleId=41785&fullArticle=true&tocId=9p41785 22.02.06
Le Goff, Jacques, *Ritter, Einhorn, Troubadoure* (Munich, 2005), 222.
Library of Congress, *World Treasures of the Library of Congress: Beginnings* (Lingfield, Surrey, 2002), 196.
Legrain, Leon, "Sumerian Sculptures," *Journal of the University of Pennsylvania Museum of Archaeology and Anthropology*, XVIII (1927), 239.
Manguel, Alberto, *A History of Reading* (New York, 1996), 226.
Meade, Marion, *Eleanor of Aquitaine: A Biography* (New York, 1977).
Okuda, Isao, e-mail correspondence with author, June-September, 2008.
Reese, Lynn, e-mail correspondence with author, 22 April 2008.
Shonagon, Sei, *The Pillow Book*, trans. Ivan Morris (New York, 1991), 13.
Spike, Michèle K., *The Tuscan Countess: The Life and Extraordinary Times of Mathilda of Canossa* (New York, 2004).
Van de Mieroop, Marc, *A History of the Ancient Near East, ca. 3000–323 BC* (Malden, MA, 2004), 66 and 69.
www.themiddleages.net/people/christine_pisan.html.07.30.06

Plates

Aruz, Joan, *The Art of the First Cities* (New York, 2003), 200.
Barnet, Peter, and Nancy Wu, *The Cloisters, Medieval Art and Architecture* (New Haven, 2007), 125.
Christiansen, Keith, *Antonello da Messina: Sicily's Renaissance Master* (New York, 2005), 15, 19.
De Caro, Stefano, *The National Archeological Museum of Naples* (Naples, 1996), 189.
De Pisan, Christine, *The Book of the City of Ladies*, trans. Jeffrey Richards (New York, 1982), 63.
Jong, Erica, *Sappho's Leap* (London, 2003), x.
Legrain, Leon, "Sumerian Sculptures," *Journal of the University of Pennsylvania Museum of Archaeology and Anthropology* XVIII (1927), 237.
Hinsch, Bret, *Women in Early Imperial China* (Boston, 2002), 124.
Murase, Miyeke, *The Tale of Genji, Legends and Paintings* (New York, 2001), ch. 50.
Okuda, Isao, e-mail correspondence with author, June-September, 2008.
Shonagon, Sei, *The Pillow Book*, trans. Ivan Morris (New York, 1991), 13.

CHAPTER 2

Ferino-Pagden, Sylvia, *Sofonisba Anguissola* (Vienna, 1995), 14.
Foister, Susan, *Holbein and England* (New Haven, 2004), 244.
http://europeanhisitory.about.com/od/schurmanmaria/Schurman_Maria.htm30.05.08
Hull, Suzanne W., *Chaste, Silent, and Obedient: English Books for Women, 1475–1640* (San Marino, 1982), 127.
Kusche, Maria, *Sofonisba Anguissola* (Vienna, 1995), 23.
Lamb, Mary Ellen, "Inventing the Early Modern Woman Reader through the World of Goods: Lyly's Gentlewoman Reader and Katherine Stubbes" in *Literacy, Authorship and Culture in the Atlantic Worlds, 1500–1800*, (Philadelphia, 2008), 17.
Manguel, Alberto, *A History of Reading* (New York, 1996) 69, 150.
Miller, Lucasta, *The Bronte Myth* (New York, 2001).
Nicoidski, Clarisse, *Die großen Malereinnen* (Munich, 1999), 122ff.
Osols-Wehden, Irmgard, *Frauen der italienischen Renaissance* (Darmstadt, 1999), 37, 68, 165, 272.
Schneider, Norbert, *The Art of the Portrait* (Cologne, 2002), 64.

Plates

Baillio, Joseph, *Elisabeth Louise Vigée Le-Brun* (Fort Worth, 1982), no. 53.
Biesboer, Pieter, et. al., *Painting in Haarlem 1500–1800: A Collection of the Frans Hals Museum* (2006), 625.
Bowron, Edgar Peters, and Mary G. Morton, *Masterworks of European Paintings in the Museum of Fine Arts* (Houston, 2000).
Cassanova, Giacomo, *The Story of my Life*, III, 10th ed. (Berlin, 1985), 237.
Dresser, Madge, Uwe. *The Regional Historian*, 2003.
Foister, Susan, *Holbein and England* (New Haven, 2004), 244.
Ferino-Pagden, Sylvia, *Sofonisba Anguissola* (Vienna, 1995), 60.
Gaunt, William, *English Paintings* (London, 1988), 75.
Gravett, Chris, e-mail correspondence with author, 21 November 2008.
Graziani, Irene, *Lavinia Fontana* (Venice, 2006).
Grooshans, Rainald, *Maerten van Heemskerk* (Berlin, 1980), 156.
Harrison, Jonathan, e-mail correspondence with author, November-December, 2008.
Homan, Potterton, *The National Gallery London* (London, 1977), 107.
Lacayo, Richard, "Making It Real," *Time Magazine* 5 May 2008, 46.
Liedtke, Walter, *Dutch Paintings in the Metropolitan Museum of Art, New York* (New Haven, 2007), 514.
Mannings, David, *Sir Joshua Reynolds: A Complete Catalogue of his Paintings* (New Haven, 2000), 400.
Munro, Jane, e-mail correspondence with author, 7 July 2008.
National Gallery of Art, information available online at www.nationalgallery.org.uk.
Quodbach Esmée, "The Age of Rembrandt, Dutch Paintings in the Metropolitan Museum," *Metropolitan Museum of Art Bulletin* (Summer 2007), 47.
Rosenthal, Michael, and Martin Myrone, *Thomas Gainsborough* (New York, 2002), 71.
Schneider, Norbert, *The Art of The Portrait* (Cologne, 1992), 64, 160.
Slive, Seymore, *Frans Hals* (Munich, 1989), 284.
Van der Osten, Gert, and Horst Keller, *Catalogue of the Paintings of the Wallraf-Richartz Museum* (Cologne, 1973), 200.
Van Suchtelen, Ariane, et. al., *Hans Holbein the Younger* (The Hague, 1943), 67.
Wheelock, Arthur K., Jr., and Ben Broos, *Johannes Vermeer* (New Haven, 1995), 190.

CHAPTER 3

Chernow, Ron, *Alexander Hamilton* (New York, 2004).
Fetterly, Judith, *Provisions: A Reader from 19th Century American Women* (Bloomington, Indiana, 1985), 8, 41.
Flanders, Judith, *Circle of Sisters* (New York, 2001), 13.
Griffin, Susan, *The Book of The Courtesans* (New York, 2001), 223.
Hackel, Heidi Brayman, and Catherine E. Kelly, *Reading Women* (Philadelphia, 2008), 109.
Oberlin College, *Alumni Register, Graduates and Former Students, Teaching and Administrative Staff 1833–1960* (Oberlin, Ohio), 1960.
Pinckney, Darryl, introduction to *Uncle Tom's Cabin* by Harriet Beecher-Stowe, 10th edition (New York, 2008), ix.
Rogers Dean M., e-mail correspondence with the author of 20 April 2009.
Slaight, Wilma R., e-mail correspondence with the author, 22 April 2009, information available online at www.archive.org/details/wellesleycollege1975well.
Staples, Roberta, e-mail correspondence with the author, 22 April 2009
Stokes, Philip, *Philosophy:100 Essential Thinkers* (New York, 2002), 109.
Taylor, Barbara, *Mary Wollstonecraft and the Feminist Imagination*, (Cambridge, 2003), 176ff.
Weinberg, Barbara H., et. al., *American Impressionism and Realism, The Painting of Modern Life, 1885–1915* (New York, 1994), 291.
Withey, Lynne, *Dearest Friend: A Life of Abigail Adams* (New York, 1981), 8.

Plates

Adler, Kathleen, and Tamar Garb, *Berthe Morisot* (Oxford, 1987), 13.
Barratt, Carrie Rebora, The Metropolitan Museum of Art New York, http://www.metmuseum.org/home.asp.
Beck, Audrey Jones, The Museum of Fine Arts, Houston, *The Collection of John A. and Audrey Jones Beck* (Houston, 1998), 108, 114.
Bowler, Ruth, Walters Art Gallery, Baltimore, painting database, e-mail correspondence with author on 4 Dec. 2008.
Boyle-Turner, Cardine, *Paul Serusier* (Ann Arbor, Michigan, 1980), 78ff.
Cikovsky, Nicolai, Jr., and Franklin Kelly, *Winslow Homer* (Washington, DC, 1995), 159.
Brooklyn Museum, *An American View – Masterpieces from the Brooklyn Museum* (New York, 2006), 104.
Buckly, Laurence, *Edmund C. Tarbell: Poet of Domesticity* (New York, 2001), 97.
Caffin, Charles H., "The Art of Edmund Tarbell," *Harpers Monthly Magazine*, June 1908, 72–73.
Cardine, Boyle-Turner, *Paul Serusier* (Ann Arbor, Michigan, 1980), 78ff.
City of Ballarat Fine Art Gallery, e-mail correspondence with the author, information available online at www.balgal.com.
Docherty, Linda J., et. al., "The Impressionist Art of Edmund C. Tarbell," *Antiques Magazine* (2001), 661/2.
Freer Gallery of Art, Smithsonian Institution, Washington, DC, Curator's label.
Griffin, Susan, *The Book of the Courtesans* (New York, 2001), 223.
Hain, Marc, *Pennsylvania Academy of the Fine Arts: 200 Years of Excellence* (Philadelphia, 2008).
Herbert, Robert L., *Impressionism: Art, Leisure, and Parisian Society* (New Haven, 1988), 28.

Kohut, Betsy, email correspondence with the author, 11 March 2009.
Lindsay, Suzanne, *Mary Cassatt and Philadelphia* (Philadelphia, 1985), pl. 29.
Lucie-Smith, Edward, *Symbolist Art* (London, 1972), 127.
Manu von Miller, "Symphony in Pink: the Portrait of Sonja Knips," *Belvedere* 1/2001: 48ff., 54, 55.
Marrese, L. M., *A Women's Kingdom, Noblewomen and the Control of Property in Russia, 1700–1861* (Ithaca, NY, 2002), p. 214.
Metropolitan Museum of Art, New York, American Wing, *A Walk Through The American Wing* (New Haven, 2001), 134.
Murphy, Patrick, email correspondence with the author, 10 April 2009.
Nygren, Edward, et. al., *Of Time and Place, American Figurative Art from the Corcoran Gallery,* (Washington, 2003), 11, 90, 94.
O'Leary, Elisabeth L. *At Beck and Call: The Representation of Domestic Servants in Nineteenth Century American Paintings* (Washington, DC, 1996), 228.
Pomeroy Jordana et. al., ed., *An Imperial Collection, Women Artists from the State Hermitage Museum* (London, 2003), 147, 158.
Roquebert Anne, *Toulouse Lautrec* (Paris, 1991), 144.
Sotheby's, *Impressionist and Modern Art Sale Catalogue*, 5 February 2007, lot 43.
Stickler, Susan, et. al. *Impressionism Transformed, The Paintings of Edmund C. Tarbell* (Hanover, 2001), 122.
Stokes, Philip, *Philosophy: 100 Essential Thinkers* (New York, 2002), 109.
Stott, Annette, *Holland Mania: The Unknown Dutch Period in American Art and Culture* (Woodstock, NY, 1998), 67.
Tyne & Wear Museum, Newcastle 2004 XHTML1.0, available online at www.twmuseums.org.uk/artonline/search.
Wallraf-Richartz-Museum, *Wilhelm Leibl* (Cologne, 1994), 343–4.
Wolk-Simon Linda, "Raphael at the Metropolitan: The Colonna Altarpiece," *The Metropolitan Museum of Art Bulletin* 10 (2006), 38.
www.voices.cla.umn.edu/vg/Bios/entries/w-heatley_phillis.html16.03.09.
www.americaslibrary.gov/jb/revold/jb_revolut_poetslav_3_e.thml.16.03.09.

CHAPTER 4

The Minneapolis Institute of Arts, *Léger's Le Grand Déjeuner* (Minneapolis, 1980) 23ff.
Söntgen, Beate, "With Downcast Eyes: Figures of Reading in the Work of Henri Matisse," in *Henri Matisse* (Düsseldorf, 2005), 85.
Schneede, Uwe M., "Munch in Deutschland," in *Edvard Munch* (Milan, 1988), 43ff.

Plates

Bischoff, Ulrich, *Edvard Munch 1863–1944* (Cologne, 1993), 74.
Eggum, Arne, *Der Linde Fries* (Lübeck, 1982), 35.
Gonzales, Ann B., San Francisco Museum of Modern Art, e-mail correspondence with author, 24 March 2009.
Goodrich, Llyod, "The War Years," in *Yasuo Kuniyoshi* (New York, 1986).
Lerheim, Karen E., e-mail correspondence with the author of 20 November 2008.
Monnier, Virginie, and Jean Clair *Baltus,* (New York, 2000), 191.
Mühren, Bas, e-mail correspondence with author, 23 July 2008.
Overland Gallery, *Semen Afanasevich Chuikov 1902–1980* (Minneapolis, 2009).
Paci, Sandra, DC Moore Gallery, NY, e-mail correspondence with author, 13 Sept 2006.
Russell, John, "Balthus, Painter Whose Suggestive Figures Caused a Stir, Is Dead at 92," *The New York Times*, 12 February 2001.
Romney, Nicole C., e-mail correspondence with author, 11 July 2008.
Smeteck, Ute, e-mail correspondence with author, 1 December 2008.
Söntgen, Beate, "With Downcast Eyes, Figures of Reading in the Work of Henri Matisse," in *Henri Matisse* (Düsseldorf, 2005), 75–78.
The Minneapolis Institute of Arts, *Léger's Le Grand Déjeuner* (Minneapolis, 1980) 23ff.
Woll, Gerd, e-mail correspondence with author, 12 May 2009.
Information from the Galeria Civica d'arte Moderna e Contemporanea, Turin available online at www.gamturino.it/descopera.php?id=53&lang=2.

List of Illustrations

Illustrations are listed by page number

© By Permission of the Master and Fellows of St. Johns College, Cambridge, Cambridge

54 Hans Holbein the Younger (1497/8–1543)
Mary, Lady Guildford, 1527
Oil on panel, 87 x 70.6 cm. (34 1/4 x 27 13/16 in.)
© Saint Louis Art Museum, Museum Purchase

58 Sofonisba Anguissola (ca. 1535–1625)
Self-Portrait, 1554
Oil on panel, 17 x 12 cm. (6 3/4 x 4 2/3 in.)
© Kunsthistorisches Museum, Vienna

65 Lavinia Fontana (1552–1614)
Widow and her Daughter, 1592–1595
Oil on canvas, 116 x 98 cm. (45 3/4 x 38 1/2 in.)
©Pinacoteca Nazionale, Bologna
Su concessione del Ministero per i Beni e le Attività Culturali

66 Gerard Dou (1613–1675)
Old Woman Reading a Bible, ca. 1630
(also called Rembrandt's Mother)
Oil on wood, 71 x 55.5 cm. (28 x 21 3/4 in.)
© Stichting Het Rijskmuseum, Amsterdam

67 Francisco de Zurbaràn (1598–1664)
Saint Margaret of Antioch, 1630–40
Oil on canvas, 163 x 105 cm. (64 1/8 x 41 1/3 in.)
© The National Gallery, London

68 Johannes Cornelisz Verspronck (1601/03–1662)
The Regentesses of the St. Elisabeth Hospital in Haarlem, 1641
Oil on canvas, 152 x 214.7 cm. (59 13/16 x 84 1/2 in.)
© Frans Hals Museum, Haarlem, Inv.no os I-622

71 Georges de La Tour (1593–1652)
The Education of the Virgin, ca. 1650
Oil on canvas, 83.8 x 100.4 cm. (33 x 39 1/2 in.)
© The Frick Collection, New York

72 Eglon van der Neer (1635/36–1703)
The Reader, ca. 1654–64
Oil on canvas, 38.1 x 27.9 cm. (15 x 11 in.)
The Metropolitan Museum of Art, The Friedsam Collection, Bequest of Michael Friedsam, 1931 (32.100.9)
Image © The Metropolitan Museum of Art

75 Johannes Vermeer (1632–1675)
Allegory of Faith, ca. 1670–72
Oil on canvas, 114.3 x 88.9 cm. (45 x 35 in.)
The Metropolitan Museum of Art, the Friedsam Collection, Bequest of Michael Friedsam, 1931 (32.100.18)
Image © The Metropolitan Museum of Art

76 Thomas Gainsborough (1727–1788)
Portrait of a Woman, ca. 1750
Oil on canvas, 75.8 x 66.7 cm. (29 7/8 x 26 1/4 in.)
© Yale Center for British Art, Paul Mellon Collection, B1977.14.55

80 Francois Boucher (1703–1770)
Resting Girl (Louise O'Murphy), 1751
Oil on canvas, 59.5 x 73.5 cm. (23 3/8 x 28 7/8 in.)
Wallraf-Richartz-Museum, Cologne, WRM 2639
Photo © Rheinisches Bildarchiv, Cologne

83 Jean-Siméon Chardin (1699–1779)
The Good Education, ca. 1753
Oil on canvas, 41.4 x 47.3 cm. (16 5/16 x 18 5/8 in.)
© The Museum of Fine Arts, Houston; Hift in memory of George R. Brown by his wife and children

84 Maurice Quentin de La Tour (1704–1788)
Mme. Ferrand Meditating on Newton, 1753
Pastel on paper, 73.5 x 60.3 cm. (30 x 23 11/16 in.)
Alte Pinakothek, Munich
Photo © Blauel/Gnamm/ARTOTHEK

87 Sir Joshua Reynolds (1723–1792)
Gertrude, Duchess of Bedford, 1756
Oil on canvas, 124.5 x 99 cm. (49 x 39 in.)
© His Grace the Duke of Bedford and the Trustees of the Bedford Estates

88 Angelica Kauffmann (1741–1807)
Louisa Hammond, ca. 1780
Oil on copper, 32.7 x 26.3 cm. (12 7/8 x 10 3/8 in.)
© Fitzwilliam Museum, Cambridge

91 Élisabeth-Louise Vigée-Le Brun (1755–1842)
Portrait of Mrs. Chinnery, 1803
Oil on canvas, 91.5 x 71 cm. (36 x 28 in.)
© 2008, Indiana University Art Museum, # 75.68,
Photo credit: Michael Cavanagh and Kevin Montague

92 Thomas Pole (1753–ca. 1829), attributed to
A View through the Window into the Garden with a Lady Writing, 14 St. James' Square, 1806
Watercolor on paper, 26.2 x 20.7 cm. (10 5/16 x 8 1/8 in.)
© Bristol's Museums, Galleries & Archives
Image © Bristol's Museums, Galleries & Archives

98 Gilbert Stuart (1755–1828)
Matilda Stoughton de Jáudenes, American, 1794
Oil on canvas, 128.6 x 100.3 cm. (50 5/8 x 39 1/2 in.)
The Metropolitan Museum of Art, New York, Rogers Fund, 1907 (07.76)
Image © The Metropolitan Museum of Art

102 Sir Edward Burne-Jones (1833–1898)
Green Summer, 1868
Oil on canvas, 64.7 x 106.1 cm. (25 1/2 x 41 3/4 in.)
Private Collection
Photo: © Bridgeman Art Library

104 Alexander Hugo Bakker Korff (1824–1882)
Bible Reading, 1879
Oil on canvas, 34 x 42 cm. (13 3/8 x 16 1/2 in.)
Gemeentemuseum, Den Haag

105 John White Alexander (1856–1915)
A Quiet Hour, ca. 1901
Oil on canvas, 122.9 x 90.5 cm. (48 3/8 x 35 5/8 in.)
© Courtesy of the Pennsylvania Academy of the Fine Arts, Philadelphia.
Josef. E. Temple Fund (Acc.no. 1904.6)

106 Rupert Charles Wulsten Bunny (1864–1947)
Woman Reading, ca. 1907
Oil on board, 52.7 x 75 cm. (20 3/4 x 29 1/2 in.)
Private Collection
Photo: Courtesy, Hirschl & Adler Galleries, New York

107 Sir John Lavery (1856–1941)
Miss Auras, The Red Book, ca. 1902
Oil on canvas, 76.3 x 63.5 cm. (30 x 25 in.)
© Philip Mould Ltd., London

109 Phillis Wheatley Writing
Cover page of her book *Poems* of 1773
Inscribed: "Phillis Wheatley, Negro Servant to Mr. John Wheatley of Boston"
Engraving by Scipio Moorhead (fl. 1770s)
Photo © Bettmann/CORBIS

110 Charles Willson Peale (1741–1827)
Mrs. Samuel Mifflin and Her Granddaughter Rebecca Mifflin Francis, American, 1777–80
Oil on canvas, 127.3 x 101 cm. (50 1/8 x 40 1/4 in.)
The Metropolitan Museum of Art, New York
Egleston Fund, 1922 (22.153.2)
Image © The Metropolitan Museum of Art

113 Ralph Earl (1751–1801)
Esther Boardman, American, 1789
Oil on canvas, 108 x 81.3 cm. (42 1/2 x 32 in.)
The Metropolitan Museum of Art, New York
Gift of Edith and Henry Noss, 1991 (1991.338)
Image © The Metropolitan Museum of Art

114 John Opie (1761–1807)
Mary Wollstonecraft (Mrs. William Godwin), ca. 1790–97
Oil on canvas, 75.9 x 63.8 cm. (29 7/8 x 25 1/8 in.)
Tate, London, © Photography 2009, Purchased 1884, No.116

117 Philippe van Bree (1786–1871)
Studio of Women Painters, ca. 1831
Oil on wood panel, 87.5 x 131 cm. (34 1/2 x 51 5/8 in.)
© Musée des Beaux Arts de Belgium, Brussels
Photo: Courtesy Hirschl & Adler Galleries, New York

118 Sir William Charles Ross (1794–1860)
Angela Georgina, Baroness Burdett-Coutts, ca. 1847
Watercolor on ivory, 41.9 x 29.2 cm. (16 1/2 x 11 1/2 in.)
© National Portrait Gallery, London

121 Christina Robertson (1796–1854)
Portrait of Grand Duchess Maria Alexandrovna, ca. 1849
Oil on canvas, 249 x 157 cm. (98 1/16 x 61 13/16 in.)
The State Hermitage Museum, St. Petersburg
Photo: © The State Hermitage Museum

122 Hans Heinrich Bebie (1800–1888)
Ladies in Conversation, 1850–55
Oil on academy board, 46.3 x 61 cm. (18 1/4 x 24 in.)
Private Collection
Photo: Courtesy Hirschl & Adler Galleries, New York

125 Gakutei Harunobu, (fl. ca. 1813–ca. 1868)
Two Geisha reading from a book, Japan, Edo period, 19th Century
Hanging Scroll, color, gold and silver on silk, 165.3 x 109.2 cm. (65 1/16 x 43 in.)
© Freer Gallery of Art, Smithsonian Institution, Washington, DC
Gift of Charles Lang Freer (F1917.234a–b)

126 Henri Fatin-Latour (1836–1904)
The Two Sisters, 1859
Oil on canvas, 98.4 x 130.5 cm. (38 3/4 x 51 3/8 in.)
© The Saint Louis Art Museum, St. Louis

127 James McNeill Whistler (1834–1903)
American
Harmony in Green and Rose: the Music Room, 1860–1861
Oil on canvas, 95.5 x 70.8 cm. (37 5/8 x 27 7/8 in.)
© Freer Gallery of Art, Smithsonian Institution, Washington, DC
Gift of Charles Lang Freer (F1898.8)

130 Sir Edward Burne-Jones (1833–1898)
Laus Veneris, 1873–75
Oil with gold paint on canvas, 122 x 183 cm. (48 x 72 in.)
© Laing Art Gallery, Tyne & Wear Museums

133 Claude Monet (1840–1926)
Springtime (La Liseuse), 1872
Oil on canvas, 50 x 65 cm. (19 11/16 x 25 9/16 in.)
© Walter Art Gallery, Baltimore

134 Berthe Morisot (1841–1895)
Reading, 1873
Oil on fabric, 46 x 71.8 cm. (18 1/8 x 28 1/4 in.)
© The Cleveland Museum of Art, Gift of Hanna Fund, 1950.89

136 Édouard Manet (1832–1883)
The Railway, 1873
Oil on canvas, 93.3 x 111.5 cm. (36 3/4 x 43 7/8 in.)
© National Gallery of Art, Washington, DC (1956.10.1) Gift of Horace Havemeyer in memory of his mother, Louisine W. Havemeyer,
Image Courtesy of the Board of Trustees of the National Gallery of Art

141 Winslow Homer (1836–1910)
The New Novel, 1877
Watercolor and gouache on paper, 24.1 x 51.9 cm. (9 1/2 x 20 in.)
© Horace P. Wright Collection, Michele and Donald D'Amour Museum of Fine Arts, Springfield, Massachusetts,
Photography by David Stansbury

142 Wilhelm Maria Hubertus Leibl (1844–1900)
Three Women in Church, 1878–1881/82
Oil on wood, 113 x 77 cm. (44 1/2 x 30 5/16 in.)
© Hamburger Kunsthalle Inv. Nr.1534
© Photo: bpk-images

145 William Merritt Chase (1849–1916)
In the Studio, ca. 1882
Oil on canvas, 72 x 124.8 cm. (28 1/16 x 49 1/8 in.)
© Brooklyn Museum 13.50

Gift of Mrs. Carll H. De Silver in memory of her husband

146 Julius LeBlanc Stewart (1855–1919)
Sarah Bernhardt and Christina Nilsson, 1883
Oil on canvas, 96.5 x 130.8 cm. (38 x 51 1/2 in.)
Private Collection
Photo © Christie's Images/The Bridgeman Art Library

149 Thomas Eakins (1844–1916)
The Artist's Wife and His Setter Dog, ca. 1884–89
Oil on canvas, 76.2 x 58.4 cm. (30 x 32 in.)
The Metropolitan Museum of Art, New York
Fletcher Fund, 1923 (23.139)
Image © The Metropolitan Museum of Art

150 Pierre Auguste Renoir (1841–1919)
The Two Sisters, 1889
Oil on canvas, 65.5 x 54.7 cm. (25 3/4 x 21 1/2 in.)
Private Collection
Photo: © Courtesy Sotheby's Picture Library

153 Henri Toulouse-Lautrec (1864–1901)
Étude (Hélène Vary), 1889
Oil on panel, 75 x 50 cm. (29 3/16 x 19 5/16 in.)
© Kunsthalle Bremen – Der Kunstverein in Bremen
Photography: Lars Lohrisch

154 Paul Sérusier (1865–1927)
Grammar (Study), 1892
Oil on canvas, 71.5 x 92 cm. (28 1/8 x 36 3/16 in.)
Musée d'Orsay, Paris
Donation de Mlle. Henriette Boutaire sous réserve d'usufruit
© RMN. Agence photographique (Musée d'Orsay RF 1981–6)/Hervé Lewandowski

157 Maurice Denis (1870–1943)
Les Muses, 1893
Oil on canvas, 171.5 x 137.5 cm. (67 1/2 x 54 1/8 in.)
Musée d'Orsay, Paris
© RMN. Agence photographique (Musée d'Orsay RF1977–139)/Hervé Lewandowski

158 Theophile van Rysselberghe (1862–1926)
Portrait of Jeanne Pissarrro, ca. 1895
Oil on canvas, 65.4 x 54.6 cm. (25 3/4 x 21 1/2 in.)
© The Museum of Fine Arts, Houston; Gift of Audrey Jones Beck

161 Cecilia Beaux (1855–1942)
New England Woman, 1895
Oil on canvas, 109.2 x 61.6 cm. (43 x 24 1/4 in.)
© Courtesy of the Pennsylvania Academy of the Fine Arts, Philadelphia. Josef. E. Temple Fund

162 Gustav Klimt (1862–1918)
Portrait of Sonja Knips, 1898
Oil on canvas, 145 x 145 cm. (57 1/16 x 57 1/16 in.)
Austrian Gallery, Belvedere, Vienna, Inv. 4403
Image © Austrian Gallery, Belvedere

165 Mary Cassatt (1844–1926).
Family Group Reading, ca. 1901
Oil on canvas, 56.5 x 122.4 cm. (22 1/4 x 44 1/4 in.)
© Philadelphia Museum of Art, No.1942–102–1
Gift of Mr. and Mrs. J. Watson Webb, 1942

166 Emanuel Phillips Fox (1865–1915)
A Love Story, 1903
Oil on canvas, 102 x 153 cm. (40 3/16 x 60 1/4 in.)
© City of Ballarat Fine Art Gallery, Ballarat, Victoria, Martha K. Pinkerton Bequest

169 Edmund Charles Tarbell (1862–1938)
Josephine and Mercie, 1908
Oil on canvas, 71.8 x 81.9 cm. (28 1/4 x 32 1/4 in.)
© Corcoran Gallery of Art, Washington, DC, Museum Purchase, Gallery Fund

173 John Singer Sargent (1856–1925)
Simplon Pass: Reading, 1911
Transparent and opaque watercolor over graphite, with wax resist, on paper, 50.8 x 35.6 cm. (20 x 14 in.)
© Museum of Fine Arts, Boston
The Hayden Collection – Charles Henry Hayden Fund, 12.214

174 Sir James Jebusa Shannon (1862–1923)
In the Dunes (Lady Shannon and Kitty), ca. 1910
Oil on canvas, 185.7 x 143.2 cm. (73 1/8 x 56 3/8 in.)
Smithsonian American Art Museum, Gift of John Gellatly

179 Max Beckmann (1884–1950)
Reclining Woman with Book and Irises, 1931
Oil on canvas, 72.5 x 116 cm. (28 1/2 x 45 2/3 in.)
Austrian Galerie Belvedere, Vienna
Image © Austrian Galerie, Belvedere

180 Gerhard Richter (b. 1932)
Lesende (Reading), 1994
Oil on linen, 72.39 x 191.92 cm. (28 1/2 x 40 1/8 in.)
San Francisco Museum of Modern Art

181 Semon Afanasevich Chuikov (1902–1980)
The Daughter of Soviet Kirghizia, 1950
Oil on canvas, 119 x 94 cm. (47 x 37 in.)
Private Collection
Photo: Courtesy Overland Gallery

183 Isaac Israels (1865–1934)
Woman Reading, ca. 1903–1907
Chalk and watercolor on paper, 50.9 x 35.3 cm. (20 1/16₄ x 13 7/8 in.)
© Collection Kröller-Müller Museum, Otterlo, The Netherlands

184 Edvard Munch (1863–1944)
Christmas in the Brothel, 1903–04
Oil on canvas, 60.5 x 88 cm. (23 13/16 x 34 2/3 in.)
Munch Museum, Oslo

187 August Macke (1887–1914)
Wife of the Artist (Study for a portrait), 1912
Oil on carton, 105 x 81 cm. (41 3/8 x 31 7/8 in.)
Staatliches Museum Preußischer Kulturbesitz, Nationalgalerie Berlin,
Image © bpk-images, Berlin

188 Fernand Léger (1881–1955)
Le Grand Déjeuner, 1921
Oil on canvas, 182 x 248 cm. (71 2/3 x 97 7/8 in.)
The Museum of Modern Art, New York
Mrs. Simon Guggenheim Fund, 1942
The Museum of Modern Art, New York
Digital Image © The Museum of Modern Art/Licensed by SCALA/Art Resource, New York

191 Gino Severini (1883–1966)
Portrait of Gina Severini (My Daughter), 1934
Oil on canvas, 100 x 73 cm. (30 3/8 x 28 3/4 in.)
© Galeria Civica d'arte Moderna e Contemporanea, Turin
Photo: © Rampazzi, 1987

193 Pablo Picasso (1881–1973)
Woman Reading, 1935
Oil on canvas, 161 x 129 cm. (63 1/8 x 50 7/8 in.)
Musée Picasso, Paris
Image © RMN/René-Gabriel Ojéda

194 Yasuo Kuniyoshi (1889–1943
Japanese/American)
I'm Tired, 1938
Oil on canvas, 102.2 x 78.7 cm. (40 1/4 x 31 in.)
© Whitney Museum of American Art, New York
Photography: Sheldon C. Collins, NY, 1996

196 Henri Matisse (1869–1954)
Reader on a Black Background, 1939
Oil on canvas, 92 x 73.5 cm. (36 1/4 x 29 in.)
Musée National d'Art Moderne – Centre Georges Pompidou, Paris
Image © CNAC/MNA.D.st. RMN

199 Balthus (1908–2001)
The Three Sisters, 1959–1964
Oil on canvas, 130 x 192 cm. (51 1/8 x 76 in.)
Private Collection

200 Pavel Fedorovich Shardakov (b. 1929)
Milkmaids, City of Volgograd, 1967
Oil on canvas, 102.9 x 206.4 cm. (40 1/2 x 81 1/4 in.)
© Courtesy of a Friend of the Springville Museum of Art, Utah

203 Roy Lichtenstein (1923–1997)
Nude Reading, 1994
Color relief print
Roy Lichtenstein Foundation, New York

204 Whitfield Lovell (b. 1959)
Salvation, 2001
Charcoal on wood, found objects, 99 x 76.2 x 19 cm. (39 x 30 x 7 1/2 in.)
Collection of Patricia and Donald Oresman
Photo: Courtesy of DC Moore Gallery, New York
© Whitfield Lovell

207 Patricia Watwood (b. 1971)
Music and Poetry, 2000
Oil on canvas, 91.4 x 152.4 cm. (36 x 60 in.)
Collection of Margaret and Gregory Hedberg, New York
© Patricia Watwood

208 Michael Glass (b. 1962)
Elizabeth Shea, 2002
Oil on canvas, 101.6 x 183 cm. (40 x 72 in.)
Collection of Dennis and Elizabeth Shea,
© Michael Glass

Back cover: Auguste Toulmouche (1829–1890)
In the Library (Les fruits défendus), 1865
Engraving/Album Maciet 174/25
© Bibliothèque des Arts Décoratifs, Paris, Collection Maciet
Image: © Suzanne Nagy, Malakoff

Bibliography

Adler, Kathleen, and Garb, Tamara. *Berthe Morisot*. Oxford, 1987.

Arnold, Bruce. *Irish Art*. London, 1977.

Bacon, Francis. *The Essays or Council Civil and Moral*. New York, 2005.

Bailey, Colin B., *Gustav Klimt, Modernism in the Making*. New York, 2001.

Banner, Lois W. *Women in Modern America: A Brief History*. 2nd ed. New York, 1984.

Barbera, Giaocchino. *Antonello da Messina, Sicily's Renaissance Master*. New Haven, 2005.

Barbier, Frèderic. "History, The Historian and Reading." *SPIEL* x (2001).

Barnhart, Richard M. *Three Thousand Years of Chinese Painting*. New Haven, 1997.

Beck, Audrey Jones. *The Collection of John A. and Audrey Jones Beck*. Houston, 1998.

Beetham, Margaret. "In Search of the Historical Reader: The Woman Reader, the Magazine and the Correspondence Column." *SPIEL* 1 (2000): 89–104.

Beetham Margaret, and Levie, Sophie. "Historical Readers and Historical Reading." *Siegener Periodicum zu internationalen empirischen Literaturwissenschaft (SPIEL)*, 19/1 (2000), special edition.

Biddle, Flora Miller. *The Whitney Women and the Museum They Made*. New York, 1999.

Bischoff, Cäcilia. *Meisterwerke der Gemäldegalerie Kunsthistorisches Museum*. Vienna, 2006.

Boskovska, G. *Die russische Frau im 17. Jahrhundert*. Cologne, 1998.

Boschoff, Ulrich. *Edvard Munch 1863–1944*. Cologne, 1993.

Bown, Matthew C. *A Dictionary of Twentieth Century Russian and Soviet Painters 1900–1980s*. London, 1998.

Bown, Matthew C. *Socialist Realist Painting*. New Haven, 1998.

Braudel, Fernand. *A History of Civilizations*. Paris, 1987.

Brayman-Hackel, Heidi, and Kelly, Catherine E. *Reading Women*. Philadelphia, 2008.

Broude, Norman. *Impressionism, A Feminist Reading*. New York, 1991.

Buckley Laurene, *Edmund C. Tarbell, Poet of Domesticity*. New York, 2001.

Cahill, Thomas. *How the Irish Saved Civilization*. London, 1995.

Cahill, Thomas. *Mysteries of the Middle Ages.* New York, 2006.
Chernow, Ron. *Alexander Hamilton.* New York, 2004.
Cikovsky, Nicolai Jr., and Kelly, Franklin. *Winslow Homer.* New Haven, 1995.
Corcoran Gallery of Art. *A Catalogue of the Collection of American Paintings in the Corcoran Gallery of Art*, vol. 2, *Painters from 1850 to 1910.* Washington, DC, 1973.
Corcoran Gallery of Art. *Of Time and Place: American Figurative Art from the Corcoran Gallery.* Washington, DC, 1981.
Crow, Thomas E. *Painters and Public Life in Eighteenth-Century Paris.* New Haven, 1985.
Currier Gallery of Art. *The Paintings of Edmund C. Tarbell.* Manchester, New Hampshire, 2001.
Christianson, Keith. "The Exalted Art of Antonello da Messina" in The Metropolitan Museum of Art, *Antonello da Messina, Sicily's Renaissance Master* (New Haven, 2005).
Cikovsky, Nicolai Jr., and Kelly, Franklin. *Winslow Homer.* New Haven, 1995.
Comini, Alessandra. *Gustav Klimt, Eros and Ethos.* Salzburg, 1975.
Crow, Thomas E. *Painters and Public Life in Eighteenth-Century Paris.* New Haven, 1985.
Curators of the American Wing, Metropolitan Museum of Art. *A Walk Through The American Wing.* New Haven, 2001.
Danly, Susan. *Light, Air and Color, American Impressionist Paintings from the Collection of the Pennsylvania Academy of Fine Arts.* Philadelphia, 1990.
Danto, Arthur C. *The Abuse of Beauty.* Peru, Illinois, 2003.
De Botton, Alain. *Status Anxiety.* New York, 2005.
De Vos, Dirk. *Rogier van der Weyden*, Munich, 1999.
Docherty, Linda J., Hirshler, Erica E., and Strickler, Susan. "The Impressionist Art of Edmund C. Tarbell," *Antiques Magazine* (November, 2001).
Dongelmans, Barry, and de Vries, Boudien. "Reading, Class and Gender: The Sources for Research on Nineteenth-Century Readers in the Netherlands," *SPIEL* 1 (2000): 56–88.
Dorival, Bernard. *L'Ecole de Paris au Musee National d'Art Moderne.* Somogy, 1961.
Dorment, Richard, and MacDonald, Margaret F. *James McNeill Whistler.* London, 1994.
Durant, Will. "Das Klassische Griechenland," in *Kulturgeschichte der Menschheit*, Will and Ariel Durant, transl. by Schneider Ernst, 1st ed. Munich, 1977.
Eggum, Arne, *The Linde Fries.* Lübeck, 1982.
Epstein, Barbara Lee. *The Politics of Domesticity: Women, Evangelicalism, and Temperance in Nineteenth-Century America.* Middletown, CT, 1981.
Evans, Sara M. *Born for Liberty: A History of Women in America.* New York, 1989.
Feist, Peter H. *Auguste Renoir.* Cologne, 1987.
Ferguson, W. *Dido's Daughters: Literacies and Ideologies of Empire in England and France, 1400–1690.* Chicago, 2003.
Fetterley, Judith. *Provisions, A Reader from 19th-Century American Women.* Indiana, 1985.
Fine Arts Museum of San Francisco. *Picasso and the War Years 1937–1945.* New York, 1998.
Flanders, Judith. *Circle of Sisters.* New York, 2001.
Flint, Kate. *The Woman Reader 1837–1914.* Oxford, 1993.
Fox, Robin Lane. "New Light on England's Lost Arcadia," *Financial Times Weekend*, March 6/7, 1993, XVII.
Fraser, Antonia. *The Six Wives of Henry VIII.* London, 1992.
The Frick Collection. *Handbook of Paintings.* New York, 1978.
Gardner, Helen. *Art Through The Ages*, 4th ed., New York, 1959.
Gaunt, Wilma. *English Painting, A Concise History*, London, 1988.
Geffrye Museum. *Home and Garden: Paintings and Drawings of English, Middle Class, Urban Domestic Spaces*, 1675 to 1914. London, 2003.
Gowing, Lawrence. *Matisse.* London, 1979.
Griffin, Susan. *The Book of the Courtesans.* New York, 2001.
Hanebutt-Benz, Eva Maria. *Die Kunst des Lesens.* Frankfurt, 1985.
Hayward Gallery. *Toulouse-Lautrec.* London, 1991.
Herbert, Robert L. *Impressionism, Art, Leisure, and Parisian Society.* New Haven, 1988.
Hind, Arthur. *An Introduction to a History of Woodcuts.* New York, 1963.
Hinsch, Bret. *Women in Early Imperial China.* Lanham, Maryland, 2002.
Hughes, Robert. *The Shock of the New.* New York, 1981.
International Cultural Corporation of Australia. *Creating Australia, 200 Years of Art, 1788–1988.* Melbourne, 1988.
James, Henry. *The Bostonians*, ed. with an introduction by Charles R. Anderson, 10th ed. London, 1984.
Jong, Erica. *Sappho's Leap.* New York, 2003.
Kent, Neil. *The Triumph of Light and Nature: Nordic Art 1740–1940.* London, 1987.
Kisluk-Grosheide Danielle O., "French Royal Furniture in The Metropolitan Museum," *The Metropolitan Museum of Art Bulletin*, Winter 2006.
Koja, Stephan, and Österreichische Galerie, Belvedere. *Nordlicht, Finnlands Aufbruch zur Moderne, 1890–1920.* Munich, 2005.
Kostenevich, A. G. *Hidden Treasures Revealed: Impressionist Masterpieces and Other Important French Paintings Preserved by the State Hermitage Museum, St. Petersburg.* New York, 1995.
Lacambre, Geneviève, et. al. *Manet, Velasquez.* Paris, 2002.
Lackner Stephan, *Max Beckmann.* New York, 1977
Leach, Maria. *The Wicked Wit of Oscar Wilde.* London, 2000.
Le Faye, Deirdre. *Jane Austen: The World of Her Novels.* London, 2002.
Le Goff, Jacques, *Ritter, Einhorn, Troubadoure.* Munich, 2005.
Leopold Museum. *Körper, Gesicht, Seele.* Vienna, 2006.
Levey, Michael. *The National Gallery Collection.* London, 1990.
Library of Congress. *Beginnings, World Treasures of The Library of Congress.* Washington, DC, 2002.
Li- Hsiang, Lisa Rosenlee. *Confucianism and Women, A Philosophical Interpretation.* New York, 2006.
Lucie-Smith, Edward. *Symbolist Art.* London, 1972.
Lyons, Deborah, and Weinberg, Adam D. *Edward Hopper and the American Imagination.* New York, 1995.
Malerei Lexikon von A bis Z. Geschichte der Malerei von den Anfängen bis zur Gegenwart. Cologne, 1986.
Manguel, Alberto. *A History of Reading.* New York, 1996.
Manguel, Alberto. *Bilder Lesen, Eine Geschichte der Liebe und des Hasses*, 2nd ed. Hamburg, 2005.
Maresse, M. L. *A Women's Kingdom: Noblewomen and the Control of Property in Russia, 1700–1861.* Ithaca, NY, 2002,
McCarthy, Kathleen D., *Women's Culture, American Philanthropy and Art, 1830–1930.* Chicago, 1991.
Meisterwerke der Österreichischen Galerie, Belvedere. Vienna, 2003.
Miller, Lucasta. *The Bronte Myth.* New York, 2001.
Mintz, Steven, and Kellogg, Susan. *Domestic Revolutions: A Social History of American Family Life.* New York, 1998.
Munro, Eleanor. *Originals – American Women Artists.* New York, 1979.
Müller, Christiane, and Kemperdick, Stephan. *Hans Holbein the Younger, The Basel Years 1515–1532*, Munich, 1943.
Murase, Miyeko. Introduction to *The Tale of Genji, Legends and Paintings.* New York, 2001.
Murray, Peter and Linda. *The Art of the Renaissance.* New York, 1995.
Musée des beaux-arts de Brest. *Autour des Symbolistes et des Nabis du musée: les peintres du rêve en Betragne.* Brest, 2006.
Museo d'Arte Moderna della Città di Lugano. *Edvard Munch.* Milan, 1998.
Museum of Modern Art, New York. *Exhibiting Matisse, Henri Matisse: A Retrospective.* New York, 1992.
National Gallery of Art, Washington and Royal Cabinet of Paintings, Mauritshuis, The Hague. *Johannes Vermeer.* Washington and The Hague, 1995.
Naumann, Ursula. *Geträumtes Glück, Angelica Kauffmann und Goethe.* Frankfurt am Main, 2007.
Nevins, Allan, and Commager, Henry Steele. *A Short History of the United States*, 6th ed. New York, 1984.
New World Encyclopedia. "Ban Zhao," available online at
http://www.newworldencyclopedia.org/entry/Ban_Zhao?oldid=678145.
Nicoidski, Clarisse. *Die großen Malerinnen, Weibliche Kunst von den Anfängen bis zur Gegenwart (Une histoire des femmes peintures).* Munich, 1999.
Nygren, Edward, Marzio, Peter C., and Myers, Julie R. *Of Time and Place, American Figurative Art from the Corcoran Gallery*, Washington, DC, 1981.
O'Leary, Elisabeth L. *At Beck and Call: The Representation of Domestic Servants in Nineteenth Century American Paintings.* Washington, DC, 1996.
Osols-Wehden, Irmgard. *Frau der italienischen Renaissance.* Darmstadt, 1999.
Peiss, Kathy. *Cheap Amusements: Working Women and Leisure in Turn-of-the Century New York.* Philadelphia, 1986.
Perry Claire, Young America, *Childhood in 19th Century Art and Culture*, New Haven 2006.
Philadelphia Museum of Art. *Masterpieces of Impressionism & Post-Impressionism, The Annenberg Collection.* Philadelphia, 1989.
Pinckney, Daryll. Introduction in Harriet Beecher Stowe's *Uncle Tom's Cabin.* New York, 2008.
Polk, Milbry, and Tiegreen, Mary. *Women of Discovery.* London, 2001.
Pomeroy, Jordana, et. al. *An Imperial Collection: Women Artists from the State Hermitage Museum.* London, 2003.
Pomeroy, Jordana, et. al. *An Imperial Collection, Women Artists from the State Hermitage Museum*, Washington, DC, 2003.
Potterton, Homan. *The National Gallery London.* London, 1977.
Prettejohn, Elizabeth. *Interpreting Sargent.* London, 1998.
Quobach, Esmée. "The Age of Rembrandt, Dutch Paintings in the Metropolitan Museum of Art." *The Metropolitan Musem of Art Bulletin*, Summer 2007.
Raynal, Maurice. *Moderne Malerei.* Geneva, 1966.
Rewald, John. *Von van Gogh bis Gauguin*, trans. by Ursula Lampe and Anni Wagner. Cologne, 1987.

Rewald, Sabine. *The Metropolitan Museum of Art, Twentieth-Century Modern Masters, The Jacques and Natasha Gelman Collection*, ed. by William S. Lieberman. New York, 1989.

Ricketts, Harry. *Rudyard Kipling*. New York, 1999.

Roberts, Cokie. *Founding Mothers – The Women Who Raised Our Nation*. New York, 2004.

Rosenthal, Angela. *Art and Sensibility*. New Haven, 2006.

Ryan, Mary P. *Cradle of the Middle Class: Family in Oneida County, New York 1790–1865*. New York, 1865.

Sandler, Irving, et. al. *Defining Modern Art, Selected Writings of Alfred H. Barr, Jr.* New York, 1986.

Schneider, Norbert. *The Art of the Portrait*. Cologne, 2002.

Schultz-Hoffmann, Carla, ed. *Max Beckmann. Retrospektive*. Munich, 1984.

Shikibu, Murasaki. *The Tale of Genji*, trans. by Richard Bowring. Cambridge, 1988.

Shonagon, Sei. *The Pillow Book*, transl. by Ivan Morris. New York, 1991.

Shorto, Russell. *The Island at the Center of the World*. New York, 2005.

Spencer, Robin. *Whistler*. London, 1990.

Städtische Galerie im Lenbachhaus. *Der Blaue Reiter im Lenbachhaus München*. Munich, 1985.

Staley, Allen. *The Pre-Raphaelite Vision*. London, 1994.

State Hermitage Museum. *French Painting from the Hermitage: Mid 19th to early 20th Century*. Leningrad, 1987.

State Hermitage Museum. *French Painting*. Leningrad, 1975.

Stein, Alyson, and Havemeyer, Lousine W. *Sixteen to Sixty, Memoirs of a Collector*. New York, 1993.

Steiner, Wendy, *Venus in Exile, The Rejection of Beauty in 20th Century Art*, New York, 2001.

Stokes, Philip. *Philosophy: 100 Essential Thinkers*. New York, 2002.

Stott, Annette. *Holland Mania, The Unknown Dutch Period in American Art and Culture*. Woodstock, New York, 1998.

Strickler, Susan, et. al. *Impressionism Transformed, The Paintings of Edmund C. Tarbell*. Manchester, NH, 2001.

Swann, Nancy Lee, *Pan Chao: Foremost Woman Scholar of China*. New York, 1932.

Sweetman, David. *Explosive Acts*. New York, 1999.

Tarnas, Richard. *The Passion of the Western Mind, Understanding the Ideas That Have Shaped our Worldview*. New York, 1991.

Taylor, Barbara. *Mary Wollstonecraft and the Feminist Imagination*. Cambridge, 2003.

The Thames and Hudson Dictionary of Art and Artists. London, 1988.

Todd, Janet. *Mary Wollstonecraft: A Revolutionary Life*. London, 2000.

Tomas, Daniel, et al. *Creating Australia, 200 Years of Art 1788–1988*. Melbourne, 1988.

Tucker, Paul-Hayes. *Monet at Argenteuil*. New Haven, 1982.

Van de Mieroop, Marc. *A History of the Ancient Near East*. Malden, MA, 2004.

Van Suchtelen, Ariane, Buvelot, Quentin, and van der Ploeg, Peter. *Hans Holbein The Younger 1497/98–1543*, The Hague, 1943.

Vigue, Jordi. *Great Masters of American Art*. New York, 2004.

Walden, Sarah. *Whistler and his Mother*. London, 2003.

Weinberg, Barbara H., et al. *American Impressionism and Realism: The Painting of Modern Life 1885–1915*. New York, 1994.

Weitzenhoffer, Frances. *The Havemeyers, Impressionism Comes to America*. New York, 1986.

Wharton, Edith, *The House of Mirth*, 10th ed. London, 1905.

Whitey, Lynne. *Dearest Friends, A Life of Abigail Adams*. New York, 2002.

UCLA Center for East Asian Studies, Lessons For Women, Ban Zhao (www.international.ucla.edu/eas/documents/banzhao.htm)

Whitney Museum of American Art. *Yasuo Kuniyoshi*. New York, 1986.

Wolf, Norbert. *Holbein*. Cologne, 2004.

Wolf, Tom. *Yasuo Kuniyoshi's Women*. New York, 1993.

Woods, Kim W., Richardson, Carlo M., and Lymberopoulou, Angeliki. *Viewing Renaissance Art*, vol. 3. New Haven, 1943.

Zhao, Ban. *The Chinese Book of Etiquette and Conduct for Women and Girls*. New York, 2008.

Zimmerman, Jean. *The Women of the House*. Orlando, FL, 2006.

Front cover: William McGregor Paxton,
The House Maid, detail. See page 211.
Back cover: Rogier van der Weyden, *The Magdalen Reading*, detail. See page 39; Sir Thomas Lawrence, *Mrs. Jens Wolff*, detail. See page 49; Edward Munch, *Christmas at the Brothel*, detail. See page 184; James Jacques Joseph Tissot, *October*, detail. See page 138.
Back flap: Auguste Toulmouche, *In the Library (Les fruits défendus)*, detail. See page 213.
Frontispiece: James Jacques Joseph Tissot, *October*, detail. See page 211.
Page 6: Agnolo Bronzino, *Laura Battiferri*, detail. See page 211.
Page 11: Rogier van der Weyden, *The Magdalen Reading*, detail. See page 39.
Page 43: Sir Thomas Lawrence, *Mrs. Jens Wolff*, detail. See page 49.
Page 95: Sir John Lavery, *Miss Auras, The Red Book*, detail. See page 107.
Page 176: Edvard Munch, *Christmas in the Brothel*, detail. See page 184.

Prestel Verlag
Königinstrasse 9
80539 Munich
Tel. +49 (0)89 24 29 08-300
Fax +49 (0)89 24 29 08-335
www.prestel.de

Prestel Publishing Ltd.
4 Bloomsbury Place
London WC1A 2QA
Tel. +44 (0)20 7323-5004
Fax +44 (0)20 7636-8004

Prestel Publishing
900 Broadway, Suite 603
New York, NY 10003
Tel. +1 (212) 995-2720
Fax +1 (212) 995-2733
www.prestel.com

Library of Congress Control Number is available: 2009929420

British Library Cataloguing-in-Publication Data: a catalogue record for this book is available from the British Library; Deutsche Nationalbibliothek holds a record of this publication in the Deutsche Nationalbibliografie; detailed bibliographical data can be found under: http://dnb.ddb.de

Prestel books are available worldwide. Please contact your nearest bookseller or one of the above addresses for information concerning your local distributor.

Project management: Anja Besserer, in collaboration with Sabine Gottswinter
Copyedited by: Cynthia Hall, Stephanskirchen
Production: Christine Groß
Art direction: Cilly Klotz
Design and layout: Lambert und Lambert, Düsseldorf
Typesetting: Setzerei Vornehm GmbH, Munich
Origination: Repro Ludwig, Zell am See, Austria
Printing & binding: Polygraf Print, Prešov

ISBN 978-3-7913-4077-7